BICYCLE
REPAIR
MANUAL

RICHARD BALLANTINE & RICHARD GRANT

DORLING KINDERSLEY, INC.
NEW YORK

A DORLING KINDERSLEY BOOK

Editors
Roddy Craig, Lol Henderson, Mary Ann Lynch, John Sargent

Designer
Sam Grimmer

Production
Louise Daly

Managing Editor
Josephine Buchanan

Managing Art Editor
Lynne Brown

First American Edition 1994

10 9 8 7 6 5 4 3 2

Dorling Kindersley Publishing, Inc., 95 Madison Avenue, New York, New York 10016

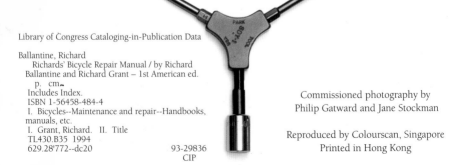

Library of Congress Cataloging-in-Publication Data

Ballantine, Richard
    Richards' Bicycle Repair Manual / by Richard
Ballantine and Richard Grant – 1st American ed.
    p. cm.
    Includes Index.
    ISBN 1-56458-484-4
    I. Bicycles--Maintenance and repair--Handbooks,
manuals, etc.
    I. Grant, Richard. II. Title
TL430.B35 1994
629.28'772--dc20   93-29836
                                    CIP

Commissioned photography by
Philip Gatward and Jane Stockman

Reproduced by Colourscan, Singapore
Printed in Hong Kong

Contents

Introduction

RIDING A BIKE IS FUN, and the better the mechanical condition of the bike, the more fun it is to ride. A bike is a mechanical extension of your body, and you can usually feel when a bike needs attention – the brakes become mushy, or gear shifts take longer. You hear odd sounds – perhaps a sticking freewheel, or the chain catching on a derailleur cage. Service your bike regularly, however, and such problems will rarely arise. Bike maintenance is easy to learn. If you are a novice mechanic, begin with simple tasks such as checking tire pressure, light lubrication, and adjusting control cables, brake blocks, saddle, handlebars, and control lever positions. In time, go on to more complex jobs such as servicing

bearings and the transmission. You'll soon become proficient, and seldom suffer the inconvenience of a breakdown. Of course, jobs such as frame repair and realignment require experience and specialized tools, and are best done by a bike shop. Most bike maintenance, however, you can do yourself. Keeping your bike in tip-top shape is very satisfying – and makes riding even more enjoyable.

Richard Ballantine

Richard Grant

Bicycle Anatomy

SPECIALIZATION HAS LED to different types of bikes, from racing bikes to mountain bikes, but basically all bikes are the same, although components vary in design, weight, and ease and method of use. A bike is made up of a frame, wheels, transmission, brakes, stem, handlebars, and saddle. Frames always bear their maker's name, but all other parts are usually supplied by different manufacturers. The precise breakdown of a bike's components is called the specification. Familiarize yourself with bike terminology; it will make repair instructions much easier to follow.

Saddle

Seat post

Micro-adjust seat bolt

Cable guide

Quick-release seat post bolt

Brake bridge

Freewheel sprockets/cogs

Cable anchor bolt

Front derailleur

Derailleur pivot bolt

Cage

Rear derailleur body

Rim

Barrel adjuster

Cable anchor bolt

Spider

Chainring

Cage

Crank dust cap

Chain

Tension pulley/wheel

Rear gear cable

Cable stop

HYBRID BIKE

The Canondale SH600 shown here is a hybrid model that blends the light weight and speed of a sport road bike with the rugged durability and versatility of a mountain bike. Perfect for riding to the office one day and exploring a muddy track the next, hybrid bikes are flexible and enjoyable – great bikes for the all-around cyclist.

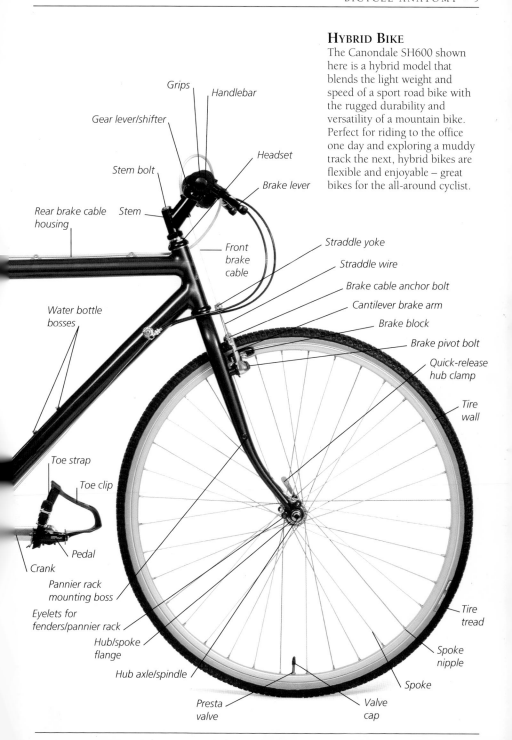

Grips

Handlebar

Gear lever/shifter

Headset

Stem bolt

Brake lever

Rear brake cable housing

Stem

Front brake cable

Straddle yoke

Straddle wire

Brake cable anchor bolt

Cantilever brake arm

Water bottle bosses

Brake block

Brake pivot bolt

Quick-release hub clamp

Tire wall

Toe strap

Toe clip

Pedal

Crank

Pannier rack mounting boss

Eyelets for fenders/pannier rack

Tire tread

Hub/spoke flange

Spoke nipple

Hub axle/spindle

Spoke

Presta valve

Valve cap

The Frame

BICYCLE FRAME DESIGN involves many interrelated elements. Slight variations produce very different characteristics and performance levels. While modern materials and technologies aid the creation of new designs, ultimately the feel and handling of a bike results from the frame-builder's own experimentation and instincts. Frames are made either from refined-ore metals, such as steel, aluminum, and titanium, or from composites of structural fibers, such as carbon, glass, or spectra, with a glue or plastic binder.

TOP TUBE
Mountain bike top tubes often slope from the head tube to the seat tube, strengthening the frame and giving the rider more clearance. Road bike top tubes tend to be more or less horizontal.

Top tube

Brake bridge

Merlin titanium mountain bike frame

Seat tube

Brazed-on cantilever brake mounting boss

Bottom bracket

FRAME GEOMETRY
Mountain bike frames are designed for off-road maneuverability and strength.The geometry (comprising the frame angles, chain-stay length, rake, and trail) is relaxed for predictable steering and stability. Road bike frames feature steeper geometry for more responsive handling.

Seat stays

Dropouts

Derailleur hanger

Chain stays

SEAT TUBE
To allow more movement under the rider when cycling over rough ground, and a low saddle on descents, the seat tube on mountain bikes is 3–5 in shorter than on the rider's road bike frame size.

CHAIN-STAY LENGTH
On mountain bikes, chain-stay length varies between 16¾ and 18½ in. Longer stays aid stability. On a racing bike the length is from 40–42 cm. This gives nimble handling but leaves no space for fenders or wide tires. Touring bikes have long chain stays to keep the rear pannier weight centered over the rear axle, and to avoid hitting the rider's heels.

BOTTOM BRACKET
The height of a mountain bike frame bottom bracket varies from 11½–13 in (29–33 cm), giving good ground clearance for obstacles. Road bike bottom brackets are usually lower, which reduces wind resistance.

FRAME SET

Bicycle tubing is made in a range of different quality grades and weights, and sold in matched frame sets for building specific bike types. Frame-builders sometimes mix tubes of different types to produce frames finely tuned to the weight and riding style of individual riders.

JOINING TECHNIQUES

Modern alloy steels are versatile and can be TIG-welded by machine or brazed (a process of joining tubes using a non-ferrous alloy such as brass, which has a lower melting point than the metals being joined). Aluminum can also be TIG-welded, or bonded with glue. The finest quality frames are still joined by hand.

Steerer tube

TITANIUM

MURDIN

WHEELBASE

The wheelbase of a bicycle frame is the distance between wheel axles, or the points where the tires contact the ground. Mountain bikes have longer wheelbases than road bikes for greater stability. The short wheelbase and steep geometry of road-racing bikes give them very fast steering reaction.

Head tube

Brazed-on cantilever brake mounting boss

Down tube

Forks

WILL THE FRAME BREAK?

Metal breaks either from an impact that exceeds its strength, or due to fatigue induced by repeated small stresses. Steel and titanium have fatigue limits and will not break if the stress is under limits. Aluminum has no fatigue limit, so each stress impact will cause weakening, and eventual failure. Aluminum frame designers acknowledge this, and incorporate enough strength for long-term safety. Even if well-worn, a steel or titanium frame will stay almost as good as new, but not aluminum frames, which generally have a useful life of three to five years. Steel frames may need to be realigned if the bike has taken a real beating. Composite frames are still too new to gauge long-term durability, but, as with aluminum, cumulative stress may lead to eventual failure.

Dropouts

FORKS

The forks on mountain bikes have to be extremely strong to endure enormous loads and successive impacts over rough terrain. It is now common to have suspension systems built into the forks for greater rider comfort and steering control. Road bike forks have to endure less shock and so can be made much lighter.

Size and Fit

THE MOST IMPORTANT feature of a bike is how it fits the rider. Performance, comfort, and the risk of injury can be affected by variations of as little as ¼ in (6 mm) in your riding position, so take care to establish your bike size and riding position. Mountain bikes are made for vigorous riding; a balanced fit that distributes the rider's weight equally is essential. Try out different bikes to get a feel of what suits you best. Stick to your correct riding position, even if it feels uncomfortable at first; the body's muscles take a little time to adapt.

Position head so front hub is obscured by handlebars when looking down

Arms should be slightly bent at elbows to allow for shock absorption, with wrists kept straight

Mountain bike riding position

Back should have forward lean of at least 45°, so stronger gluteus muscles in buttocks and lower back can be used for pedaling power. Keep back straight for easy breathing

When riding, widest part of foot should be directly over pedal axle. Rider's weight should be centered between the wheels

RACING BIKE POSITION

To achieve the optimum racing bike riding position, make sure you have the correct drop handlebar extension. Too short an extension causes the back to arch, compressing the diaphragm and impairing aerobic cycling performance. Too long an extension results in locked elbows and back strain. With the saddle at the correct height, 3½–5 in (9–13 cm) of seat post should be exposed. Keep your body forward when riding on the flat, and shift your weight back when climbing. This gives additional pedaling power.

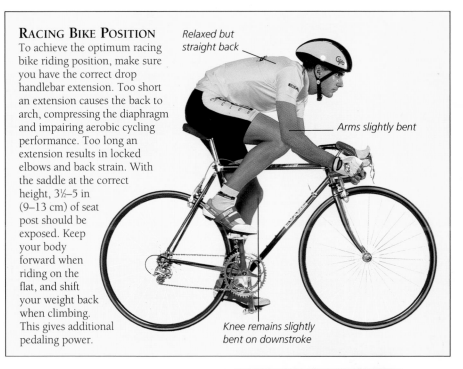

Relaxed but straight back

Arms slightly bent

Knee remains slightly bent on downstroke

FITTING THE BIKE TO THE RIDER

For mountain biking and racing, a rider should use the smallest frame that fits. Small frames save weight and are stiffer and more responsive. For touring, a larger frame provides more stability on descents and corners. The vital factors in sizing a bike are saddle height (see p.14), the length of the top tube, the amount of seat post exposed when the saddle height is correct, and the clearance between your crotch and the top tube. These factors will vary depending on the type of bike and the rider's own physique. Standard advice on sizing a mountain bike recommends that the bike be 2–4 in (5–10 cm) smaller than the rider's road bike frame size. For safety, you need to be able to move the bike around beneath you without bashing your thighs, and to have the confidence to take a fall without serious injury, so a smaller frame makes sense.

Top tube

CROTCH TO TOP TUBE CLEARANCE

The bike shown above is too big for the rider. For off-road riding, there should be at least 3–4 in (8–10 cm) clearance between the rider's crotch and the top tube, and at least 1 in (2.5 cm) clearance for commuting or touring.

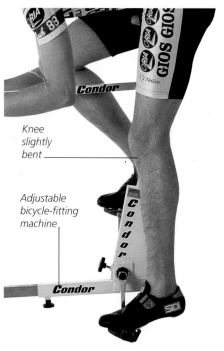

Knee
slightly
bent

Adjustable
bicycle-fitting
machine

CHECK SADDLE HEIGHT

Make the following quick and simple checks to find out whether your saddle is at the right height: first, sitting on the saddle with the ball of your foot on the pedal and the pedal down, your knee should be slightly bent (left); secondly, if you can feel your hips rocking from side to side when pedaling, your saddle is too high, and should be adjusted.

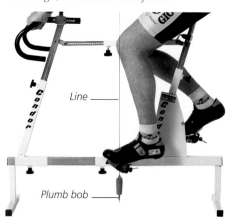

Line

Plumb bob

FORE AND AFT POSITION OF SADDLE

Sit on the saddle with both cranks parallel to the ground. Using a plumb bob line, move the saddle backward or forward until the line between the bony part of your knee and the center of the pedal axle matches the plumb bob line. Secure the saddle in this postion. From this point, you can set the saddle ⅜ in (1 cm) forward for high cadence (pedaling rate), and ⅜–¾ in (1–2 cm) back for power.

SADDLE TILT

To alter saddle tilt, you need to adjust the angle of the seat clamp. Conventional seat clamp bolts (right) are adjusted with wrenches, while micro-adjust seat clamp bolts (far right) are adjusted with a 6 mm Allen key. First use a level (above) to set the saddle in a completely level position. Now try the saddle out. Lower the saddle nose slightly if the saddle feels awkward. Lowering the saddle too far will strain your arms and back. Setting the nose too high will also eventually cause discomfort.

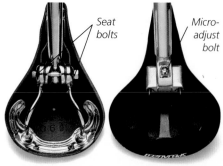

Seat
bolts

Micro-
adjust
bolt

Conventional seat clamp   Micro-adjust seat clamp

STEM HEIGHT

On a racing bike, the height of the stem should position the handlebars 1–3 in (2.5–7.6 cm) below the saddle, and 1–2 in (2.5–5 cm) below the saddle on a mountain bike. To adjust stem height on all bikes, loosen the stem bolt, then tap it with a hammer and wooden block to dislodge the stem. Grease the stem and replace it at the correct height. (Most stems have a mark indicating maximum safe extension.) Tighten the stem bolt firmly. The handlebars should be secure but able to move if the bike falls.

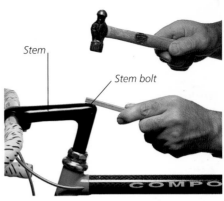

Stem

Stem bolt

COMPO

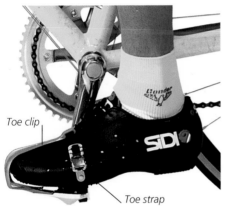

Toe clip

Toe strap

PEDALS

Always pedal with the widest part of your foot over the pedal axle for the most riding power. Make sure there is a gap of at least 3/16 in (5 mm) between the tips of your shoes and your toe clips. If you use slotted cleat or step-in clipless pedals, align the cleats with the natural rotation of your feet. Loosen the cleat mounting bolts so the cleats will move as your feet twist. Ride in various positions until you feel most comfortable. Lift slotted cleats off carefully and tighten the mounting bolts. Ask a friend to tighten the bolts on clipless pedals, because disengaging your feet will disturb the cleats.

HANDLEBARS

Mountain bike handlebar widths range from 21–24 in, and should be at least as wide as your shoulders. (The range for road bars is 38–44 cm.) Wider bars give better slow-speed control (vital for off-road riding); narrower bars suit racing and sqeezing through tight gaps in traffic. Brake levers should always be positioned correctly to reduce strain on hands and forearms.

Brake lever housing

RACING BIKE BRAKES

Position brake lever mounts so the tips of the levers just touch a straightedge laid along the handlebar end.

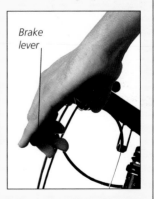

Brake lever

MOUNTAIN BIKE BRAKES

The key to correct mountain bike brake lever position is a straight wrist. Brake using middle and index fingers only.

Tools for the Job

THE KEY TO EFFECTIVE bike maintenance and repair is good organization. Find a comfortable, well-lit, and preferably warm space to work in, with a workbench or table. You will also need a means to hold the bike up with the wheels off the ground, the right tools for your type of bike and components, parts if necessary, cleaning equipment, and lubricants required for the job. Use good-quality tools made for the specific parts. Cheap tools are frustrating to use (they may be made of inferior metals that bend under stress), and they can damage a bike. Keep your tools in toolboxes so you know where everything is, especially your 2 mm Allen keys! It is also worth investing in an economical bike stand like those shown below; being able to turn the back wheel and cranks makes working on the transmission much easier. If you have several bikes, an advanced workstand (see p.19) is worthwhile – or share one with friends.

Adjuster

Chain stay hook

Clamp

Height adjuster

TRIPOD STAND

The Kestrel Trio is a simple, inexpensive stand that holds the bike by the stays, permitting transmission adjustments and removal of the rear wheel. Light and portable, it can also serve as a convenient parking stand.

WORKBENCH STAND

Most workbench manufacturers include a stand such as the Kestrel, which can be clamped onto a vise-grip type workbench. The stand lifts the bike to a comfortable height, so that you can stand up as you work on it.

HOME WORKSHOP

The tools pictured here are the basic essentials of your home workshop. Invest in good-quality tools; you do not need many, and good tools are much easier to work with. Some of the tools are bike-specific, and should be available at most good bike shops. Those tools that are not bike-specific should be available at your local hardware or auto store. Some of the tools are reasonably lightweight and can be carried on a long ride. If you are riding in a group, carry one set for everyone to use.

Y-socket tool is a handy combined tool with 8 mm, 9 mm, and 10 mm sockets

Cable cutter will cut through cable wire and cable housing

Pin wrenches are lightweight and are used for gaining access to bottom brackets

Crank extractor has to match or be made by the same manufacturer as your cranks. You cannot remove your cranks without one

Allen (hex) keys are essential bike tools. Six sizes (2 mm, 2.5 mm, 3 mm, 4 mm, 5 mm, and 6 mm) should cover most of your needs

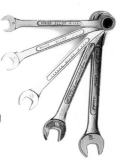

Spoke key is used for replacing and tensioning spokes

Chain tool is essential for chain adjustments. If you have a unique chain, you will need a matching chain tool

Ring wrenches (right and above right) are useful tools. Equip yourself with a range of sizes: 8 mm, 9 mm, 10 mm, 11 mm, 12 mm, 13 mm, 14 mm, 15 mm, 16 mm, and 17 mm

Cone wrenches – the two essential sizes are 13/14 mm and 15/16 mm. Have at least two of each size

Large screwdriver is handy to use as a lever

Adjustable wrenches – 4 in and 6 in sizes are useful and easy to carry around. Avoid cheap varieties

PROFESSIONAL TOOLS

The tools illustrated here are specialized, well made from strong materials, and designed for extremely effective and repeated use. Professional-quality tools are used constantly by full-time bike mechanics for every job, so they are engineered for ease and comfort of use, and complete dependability. Unfortunately, tools such as these tend to be expensive, with the exception of the freewheel remover, and worth the investment only if you ride frequently and enjoy servicing your bike regularly. Use your tools carefully, to avoid overtightening bolts and stripping threads.

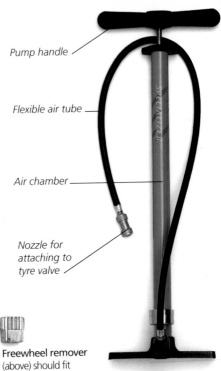

Pump handle

Flexible air tube

Air chamber

Nozzle for attaching to tyre valve

Ratchet wrench

Fixed cup and pin wrench

PARK HCW4 USA

Headset and pedal wrench

32 MM PARK HC   USA   MM

Headset and lockring wrench

36 MM PARK HCW10 USA

Lockring and headset wrench

CAMPAGNOLO

Lockring wrench

VAR

Specialized wrenches like those above are great to use and will not bend, get damaged, or, more to the point, will not damage any of your bike parts

Freewheel remover (above) should fit your freewheel exactly, otherwise the remover could cause damage

Track pump – a heavy-duty pump with a bigger chamber than a hand pump – makes inflating tires quick and effective

Deluxe crank extractor has a built-in handle for convenience

Bench vise – although not a bike-specific tool, a bench vise is very useful as a means of securing parts of a bike while you work on them. The vise should be clamped to a workbench or sturdy wooden table

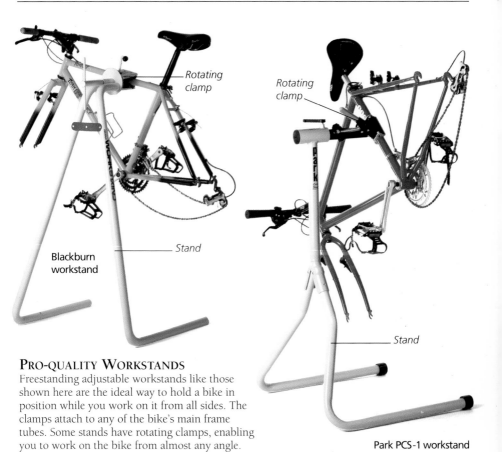

Rotating clamp

Rotating clamp

Stand

Blackburn workstand

Stand

PRO-QUALITY WORKSTANDS

Freestanding adjustable workstands like those shown here are the ideal way to hold a bike in position while you work on it from all sides. The clamps attach to any of the bike's main frame tubes. Some stands have rotating clamps, enabling you to work on the bike from almost any angle.

Park PCS-1 workstand

MULTITOOLS

The bike-specific combination tools shown here are lightweight and compact. They are the ideal tools to include in a basic contingency tool kit; the variety of sockets and removable heads included in them should cover most of the adjustments you may need to make while out on a ride.

Multisocket palm tool is a multipurpose tool with detachable Allen key and screwdriver heads, and a range of socket sizes between 8 mm and 14 mm

Cool Tool comprises Allen keys, cone wrench, crank tool, chain breaker, headset wrench, and bottom bracket tool

Six-in-one tool has Phillips and flat-blade screwdrivers, with 3 mm, 4 mm, 5 mm, and 6 mm Allen keys

Brakes

A WIDE VARIETY OF BRAKE systems are available, including drum and disc brakes, which work on wheel hubs. The most common are cable-activated caliper brakes (cantilever, side-pull, and center-pull brakes), which work on the rim. There are also advanced hydraulic-activated caliper brakes. Before servicing your brakes, always make the following basic checks. First, ensure the rims are true (see pp.32–33) and in good condition; if they are streaked and dirty, clean them with steel wool. Check the brake blocks for wear, removing any grit. Inspect the cables and cable housing for damage. Replace any old or suspect components. After servicing brakes, test with hard braking: transfer your body weight to the pedals as soon as you brake, lifting your rear end backward out of the saddle. Apply the rear and front brakes just short of skidding or being thrown over the handlebars.

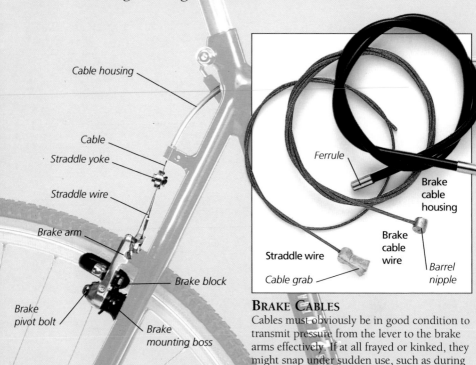

Cable housing

Cable

Straddle yoke

Straddle wire

Brake arm

Brake block

Brake pivot bolt

Brake mounting boss

Ferrule

Brake cable housing

Brake cable wire

Straddle wire

Cable grab

Barrel nipple

BRAKE CABLES

Cables must obviously be in good condition to transmit pressure from the lever to the brake arms effectively. If at all frayed or kinked, they might snap under sudden use, such as during an emergency stop. Make sure you buy cables with the correct diameter and type of nipple for your brake lever, typically pear nipples for road brakes and barrel nipples for cantilevers.

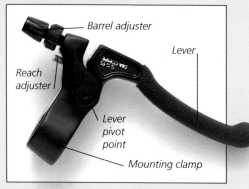

- Barrel adjuster
- Lever
- Reach adjuster
- Lever pivot point
- Mounting clamp

BRAKE LEVERS

Mountain bike brake levers come in two- or four-finger designs, and are fitted with barrel (cable) and reach adjusters. Position brake levers pointing slightly down from the handlebars, so that two fingers can rest on them constantly, while the wrist remains straight.

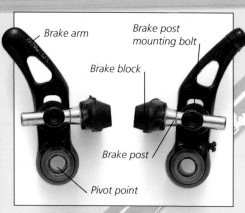

- Brake arm
- Brake post mounting bolt
- Brake block
- Brake post
- Pivot point

CANTILEVER BRAKES

Although cantilever brakes vary in design, the basic mechanics are the same. All are rigidly mounted on bosses integral to the forks or stays, which place them near the wheel rims and thus improves performance. Recent "in-board" cantilever designs feature steeply angled brake arms, giving cleaner lines without sacrificing performance.

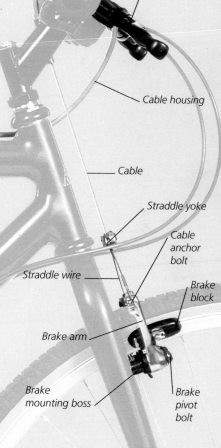

- Brake lever
- Cable housing
- Cable
- Straddle yoke
- Cable anchor bolt
- Straddle wire
- Brake block
- Brake arm
- Brake mounting boss
- Brake pivot bolt

Cable Changes

SMOOTH-RUNNING, WELL-LUBRICATED cables are essential for sensitive bike control. You will find that regular servicing and replacement make cable breakages a rare occurrence. For brakes, especially on mountain bikes and hybrids, use the thickest cables your system will accept. Thicker cables are stronger and less likely to stretch and they have a positive and responsive feel. Brake and gear changing cable systems vary from bike to bike, but their maintenance is basically similar. In the U.S., the right-hand lever is used for the rear brake. In Britain and many other countries, the left-hand lever is used.

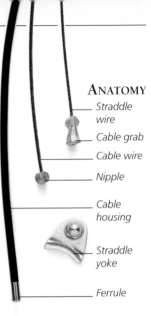

ANATOMY

Straddle wire

Cable grab

Cable wire

Nipple

Cable housing

Straddle yoke

Ferrule

CABLE CUTTING

Do not cut off any excess cable wire until it has been threaded through the housing and the cable anchor bolt. (Cutting can cause the end of the wire to splay, making it difficult to thread.)

TRIMMING CABLE HOUSING

Cut the exterior vinyl sheath with a knife to expose the metal housing, then trim it to fit between the guides on the frame.

THE RIGHT TOOLS

Use good-quality wire cutters – pliers will fray the cable. Never saw through the cable; for a clean edge, snap the cutters shut sharply.

CABLE ENDS

When the cable wire has been installed and the excess trimmed, crimp a cable end-cap onto the end with pliers to stop it fraying.

FITTING A NEW CABLE – CANTILEVER BRAKES

1 ATTACH CABLE TO BRAKE LEVER

Insert the cable wire nipple into the brake lever, and nest the cable housing securely in the barrel adjuster. Run the cable through the guides fitted to the frame – these vary from bike to bike – down to the straddle yoke.

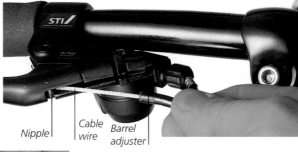

Nipple | Cable wire | Barrel adjuster

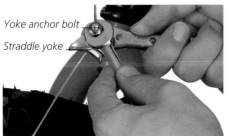

Yoke anchor bolt
Straddle yoke

2 CONNECT THE STRADDLE YOKE

Make sure the ends of the cable housing are securely fitted in their stops. Thread the wire through the small hole in the yoke anchor bolt. Holding the bolt still with a 10 mm wrench (if the bolt turns, the wire may kink), tighten the yoke anchor nut. Do this before connecting the straddle wire. The yoke height alters the angle between the straddle wire and brake arms; this angle affects braking character (see p.25).

Straddle wire

Brake arm pinch bolt

3 CONNECT THE STRADDLE WIRE

Slot the straddle wire grab end into the brake arm seat, then pass the wire through the U-shaped groove in the yoke and thread it through the pinch bolt on the opposite brake arm. Keeping the brake blocks pressed against the rim, take up the slack in the wire by pulling it through the pinch bolt. Now tighten the pinch bolt. New cables should be stretched and a final brake adjustment made (see p.25).

ALTERNATIVE STRADDLES

There are a number of small variations in straddle system design. The recent Shimano type shown here dispenses with the need for the cable wire to be clamped at the straddle yoke. The grab end of the small straddle wire slots into the brake arm seat. The cable wire is then threaded through the yoke and the small sleeve that extends from it. The end of the cable wire is then pulled through and tightened at the pinch bolt (taking up the slack as in Step 3, above). This system has the advantage of automatically setting the straddle at the correct angle for optimum brake performance.

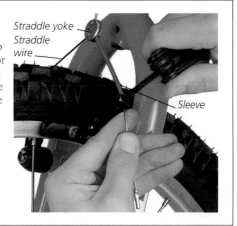

Straddle yoke
Straddle wire

Sleeve

Brake Blocks

THE IMPORTANCE OF HAVING correctly positioned
and well-maintained brake blocks cannot be
underestimated, especially if you ride a lot in
wet and muddy conditions. This applies to all
brakes. Faulty brakes could result in a bad
accident, so check, adjust, and service them
regularly. Brake block adjustment can be tricky,
and inevitably there is a lot of trial and error
involved, but it is worth being as precise as
you can be. A wide variety of brake blocks are
available, from traditional rubber blocks to
hard, high-friction synthetic blocks. Remember
always to replace brake blocks in pairs.

ANATOMY

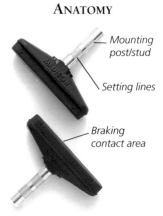

Mounting
post/stud

Setting lines

Braking
contact area

Pair of Aztec brake blocks

Shimano
M-system
brake block

Scott/Mathauser
"superbrake" block

HIGH-PERFORMANCE BRAKE BLOCKS

The Shimano and Scott/Mathauser brake
blocks shown here are extremely effective
in the wet. The Scott/Mathauser block has a
relatively small contact area, but is made of
very hard rubber, while the Shimano block
compensates for using a softer rubber by
having a large braking contact area. Some
long blocks are manufactured with a curve
that matches the contour of the wheel rim.

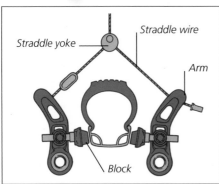

Straddle yoke

Straddle wire

Arm

Block

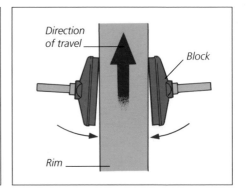

Direction
of travel

Block

Rim

BRAKE BLOCK POSITION

When activated, brake blocks must press
accurately against the wheel rim, as shown
above. If they are too low on the rim, they
could slip and impede the spokes; if too high,
they may dig into the tire.

BRAKE BLOCK TOE-IN

Slight slack in the cantilever mechanism allows
brake blocks to twist a little when activated. To
compensate, there should be a ¹⁄₁₆ in (1 mm)
gap between the rim and the rear of a block
when the front of the block is touching the rim.

CANTILEVER BRAKE BLOCK ADJUSTMENT

1 POSITION BLOCKS
Loosen each block locknut with a wrench to allow manual adjustment. Position each block relative to the wheel rim. Use the setting lines on the block mounting posts to set the blocks evenly. With the appropriate Allen key, hold the blocks in place while retightening the locknut. This secures them in their optimum position. Apply brake levers to test, and readjust if necessary.

2 CENTER BRAKES
Cantilever brake tension should be distributed equally (centered) between both brake arms. Shimano cantilever brakes are easily centered by means of a small centering screw embedded in the right-hand side of one brake arm only. Adjust the screw using a 2 mm Allen key. Test the tension by pulling on the brake levers. Readjust the centering screw if necessary.

BRAKE SERVICING

Cantilever brake arms pivot on bosses that need to be kept clean and greased. If a boss is scarred, smooth it with emery paper and steel wool. Do this lightly; if you make the boss smaller, the brake arm will fit loosely and hamper performance. When replacing brake arms, do not tighten pivot bolts too much, as this can cause binding.

BRAKE ARM REMOVAL
Once the straddle wire is disengaged, reducing tension on the brake arms, undo the pivot mounting bolts with an Allen key to remove the arms.

SPRING TENSION
The choice of hole on the brake arm boss dictates the tension in the brake arm spring. Use more tension in muddy or wintry conditions.

Road Brakes

THE BRAKE SYSTEMS used on
lightweight road-racing bikes are
usually cable-activated side-pull
caliper-action brakes with single or
dual pivot points. Side-pull brakes
combine light weight with precise
performance, and work effectively
on lightweight racing bikes, but are
not suited to heavily laden touring
and commuting bikes, which are
typically equipped with center-pull
or cantilever brakes.

ANATOMY

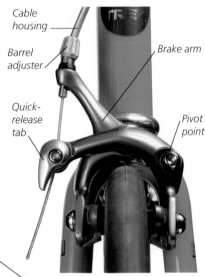

Cable
housing

Barrel
adjuster

Quick-
release
tab

Brake arm

Pivot
point

SIDE-PULL CABLE CHANGE

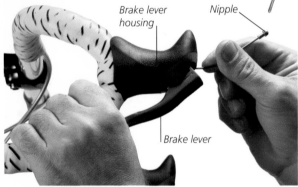

Brake lever
housing

Nipple

Brake lever

1 REMOVE CABLE
Turn the barrel adjuster
all the way clockwise. Undo
the cable anchor bolt with an
Allen key. Remove the cable
end-cap, depress the brake
lever, and extract the cable
wire. Replace the cable
housing if it is damaged or
frayed (see p.44).

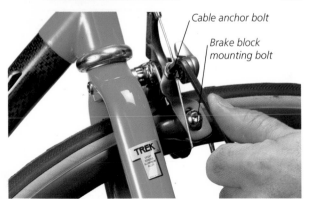

Cable anchor bolt

Brake block
mounting bolt

2 REPLACE CABLE
Once greased, thread the
new cable wire through the
brake lever and cable housing,
rotating it to keep the strands
from fraying. Seat the wire in
the anchor bolt and tighten it
firmly. Close the quick-release
tab and depress the brake lever
one or two times to stretch the
cable. If there is still play, keep
the caliper arm compressed
against the wheel rim, then
undo and reset the anchor bolt.

CALIPER ADJUSTMENT

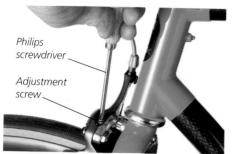

Philips screwdriver

Adjustment screw

1 CENTER BRAKES

Both brake blocks should strike the rim at the same time, which requires the caliper action of the brakes to be centered. For Shimano dual pivot bolt brakes, center brakes by adjusting the centering adjustment screw as shown. To center single pivot bolt brakes, undo the pivot bolt nut behind the forks, then position and hold the brake arms steady while retightening the bolt.

2 FINE-TUNE BRAKES

If there is any play or binding in the brakes (both dual pivot and single pivot types), adjust the pivot bolts. Undo locknuts with a wrench, tighten the pivot bolts clockwise, then reverse them slightly. Hold bolts in place with an Allen key and redo locknuts. Check brake action and readjust if you need to. Periodically disassemble, clean, and grease pivot bolts.

TREK

BRAKE BLOCK SET-UP

All side-pull brake blocks have a single mounting bolt. Undo the locknuts to position the blocks. Be sure locknuts do not twist the blocks out of line when redone. If blocks do twist, undo the nuts and set blocks slightly askew. Redo nuts.

Locknut

TOE-IN WITH WASHER

Toe-in cannot normally be adjusted on side-pull brakes. You can, however, use a dished or shaped washer in the brake block mounting bolt set-up. Set the washer in a position where it alters the angle at which the block will strike the wheel rim.

Washer

Dished washer

Brake block

Brake arm

TRADITIONAL TOE-IN METHOD

This effective traditional method involves manually bending the brake arms with an adjustable wrench in one smooth movement. Ensure that the jaws of the wrench grip the brake arm firmly. There is a risk of metal fatigue, so practice the technique with caution.

Wheels and Tires

A BICYCLE WHEEL IS A SOPHISTICATED engineering design, and despite its light weight and the relative weakness of its individual parts, it is an incredibly strong structure. The tension of the spokes, which are usually made of stainless steel, pulls, or compresses, the wheel rim inward toward the center of the wheel, and this is the secret of the wheel's strength. Different arrangements of spoke patterns, for example, two-, three-, and four-cross tangential patterns, are used to increase the strength of the wheel's resistance to pedaling and braking forces. The rims are also designed to provide the primary surface for braking and are hollow in cross-section (similar to box girders), which enhances strength but is also lightweight. Never underestimate the importance of keeping wheels true and well maintained – a faulty wheel can be potentially lethal. So check wheels and tires thoroughly before every ride.

Rim

Nipple

Tire wall

Spoke

Tread

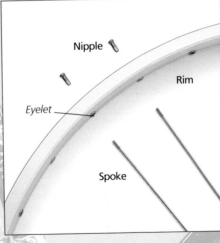

Nipple

Rim

Eyelet

Spoke

RIMS AND SPOKES

Good bike rims have eyelets that prevent the spoke nipples from jumping through the rim. Spokes should always be evenly tensioned on each side of the wheel for the wheel to be true (see pp.32–33). Measure an old spoke accurately, or take one with you when you are buying new ones at a bike shop, as they come in hundreds of different lengths. Your tool kit should always include a spoke key.

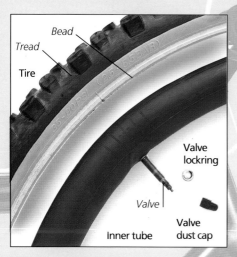

Bead
Tread
Tire
Valve lockring
Valve
Inner tube
Valve dust cap

TIRES AND TUBES

There is now a bewildering array of bike tires on the market, especially for mountain bikes. For optimum performance and durability, ensure that the width of the tires you buy matches the width of your rims. When you replace tubes, take an old one to the bike shop with you, and make sure you buy tubes with the correct type of valve fitted. To save having to mend a puncture when you are out on a ride, always carry a spare inner tube with you.

Braking surface

Tread

Tire wall

Rim

Nipple

Spoke

Spokes and Truing

BIKE WHEELS USUALLY have 32 or 36 spokes and are built using radial or, most commonly, tangential spoke arrangements. The spokes in a radial pattern, which is rare on production bikes, literally radiate from the hub to the rim, making the wheel light with minimal wind resistance (drag). In a tangential pattern the spokes cross over each other obliquely (as in the photos below), so that torque is better transmitted from acceleration or braking. Spokes are made from steel: chrome- or nickel-plated, galvanized rustless, or stainless.

ANATOMY

Spoke nipple

Thread

Plain gauge spoke

SPOKE THICKNESS

Spokes are available in butted and nonbutted (plain gauge) form. Butted spokes are thicker at the ends than in the middle, making the wheel lighter and more resilient.

REPLACING A DAMAGED OR BROKEN SPOKE

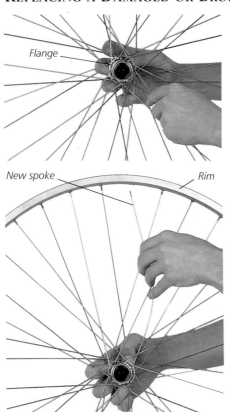

Flange

New spoke   *Rim*

1 INSERT NEW SPOKE
First take the tire and tube off the wheel. Remove rim tape from inside the rim if there is any. If the spoke is damaged but still intact, unscrew the nipple and pull the spoke out at the hub flange. If the spoke is broken, remove any fragments at each end. Push the end of the new spoke through the empty eye in the flange – this may mean coming through the wheel from the other side, as the spokes run alternately to the inside and the outside of the flange – until the elbow and spoke head catch.

2 THREAD NEW SPOKE
Examine how the spokes are laced in relation to each other, according to the tangential spoke arrangement. With the spoke head flush with the flange, weave the spoke into place, copying the arrangement of the second spoke along (alternate spokes follow the same lacing pattern). Do not force the spoke – it should flex quite easily if you apply gentle pressure.

Elbow

Spoke head

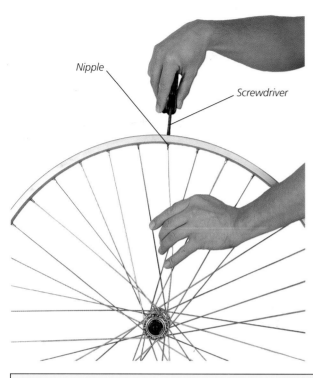

Nipple

Screwdriver

3 TENSION SPOKE
Thread the end of the spoke through the eyelet in the rim, then push the nipple onto the end. Oil the nipple with a light penetrating lubricant to prevent the nipple and the spoke thread from binding. Screw the nipple onto the spoke with a screwdriver. Tighten the spoke to approximately the same tension as the other spokes on the wheel. File down any spoke ends protruding into the rim.

4 TRUE THE WHEEL
Unless the wheel is virtually brand-new, replacing a damaged or broken spoke will inevitably put the wheel out of true. Follow the procedures for assessing how much a wheel is out of true and then for truing it, as described on pp.32–33.

SPOKELESS WHEELS
Wheels are made with spokes to save weight. However, as the wheels spin, the spokes churn the air, generating aerodynamic drag. To overcome drag, designers have created wheels like the disc wheel and the tri-spoke wheel, which smooth the flow of air. Although heavier than spoked wheels, these wheels are much faster and require less energy at high speeds. Disc wheels are only used at the rear, where they are effectively shielded by the rider's legs and the frame tubes – at the front, they would act like a sail, making the bike very difficult to handle. The spokes on tri-spoke wheels act like airfoils, and tri-spokes are used at both the front and rear.

Disc wheel

Tri-spoke wheel

CHECKING THE WHEELS

CHECKING WHEELS FOR TRUING

Wheel truing is an art more than a science, so as a beginner you should not expect perfection on your first attempt. Each spoke should be checked for bends and breaks. Check for even tension by plucking the mid-point of each spoke and listening to the note produced. Front wheel spokes should all sound the same if the tension is even all around. On the rear wheel, the spokes on the freewheel side of the hub have more tension than the spokes opposite. If any are too tight, loosen them until they feel and sound the same as the others on the same side.

TRACKING

An important step when examining your bike wheels is to check the tracking. This simply means checking the alignment of the wheels relative to each other, along a center line dictated by the top tube. Turn the bike upside down so it rests on its saddle and handlebars. Make sure the handlebars are set straight ahead. Sit behind one of the wheels so that, at eye level, you can see whether the wheels are in line. (See also p.86.)

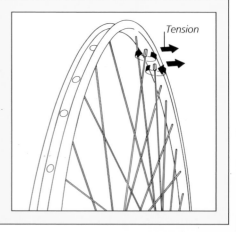

Top tube

BALANCING TENSION AT THE RIM

Obtaining even tension on front wheel rims is easier than rear wheel rims, because the spokes on both sides of the front wheel hub are at the same angle, and tensioned equally in order to keep the rim central. Back wheel rims also run centrally, but over the length of the hub and freewheel. The flange on the freewheel side of the wheel is not at the edge of the hub, so there are different spoke angles on either side of the wheel, giving a dish shape. To ensure equal rim tension, work a ½ turn at a time, balancing each side. If you loosen one spoke by a ½ turn, tighten its opposite by the same amount.

Tension

TRUING A WHEEL

Chalk

1 MARK UP THE WHEEL

Mark lateral high spots (points where the rim is most out of true) by holding chalk or a marker against one of the stays while the wheel is spinning. Slowly bring the chalk in until it comes into contact with the high points on the rim. The longest mark made by the chalk indicates the area where the spokes need adjusting first.

2 LATERALLY ADJUST

Even tension is vital, so adjust any spoke in the marked area that is out. Loosen the spokes that lead to the hub flange on the same side as the mark; tighten those leading to the opposite flange. Spin the wheel to check progress. With the first mark corrected, move to the next longest mark.

Spoke key

WHEEL STANDS

If possible, use a wheel stand to check and true wheels. Faults can be better measured and adjusted than rough-truing using the dropouts. Wheel stands have adjustable reference pointers that help you judge lateral and vertical truth.

Base

Lateral truth pointer

Vertical truth pointer

Chalk mark indicates lateral high spot

3 VERTICALLY ADJUST

Mark vertical high spots by holding a marker over the top of the rim and spinning the wheel. Where there are high spots, tighten the spokes in groups of four; with flat spots, loosen the spokes. Work slowly, tightening spokes only a little at a time for accuracy.

4 FINE-TUNE ADJUSTMENTS

After making any vertical adjustments, check again for side-to-side play, and correct by adjusting the spokes again if necessary. Remove any rim tape from the inside of the rim and look for protruding spokes that might puncture the inner tube. File these down before replacing the rim tape.

Tires and Tubes

DEPENDING ON WHAT TYPE of cycling you enjoy most, it is worth experimenting with different types of tires. Mountain bike tires are usually measured in inches, and road tires either in inches or metrically. The most common mountain bike tire size is 26 inches in diameter, with tread widths varying from 1–2.7 in. When you choose a tire at a bike shop, pick one that is easy to take off your bike rim. Also keep a stock of right-size inner tubes on hand.

ANATOMY

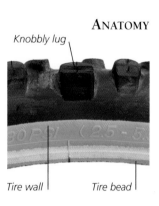

Knobbly lug

Tire wall | Tire bead |

Treadless slick tire

Multipurpose Nimbus tire

Knobbly rear tire

DIFFERENT TREAD PATTERNS

The three types of mountain bike tire tread patterns shown here are the most commonly available ones for different conditions of use. The treadless slick provides optimal grip on asphalt and concrete, giving a comfortable ride with minimal rolling resistance and low tire noise. The multipurpose Nimbus tire is a lightweight all-around performance tire that is very stable in wet weather. It is suitable for hard-packed off-road surfaces, but not mud. The knobbly rear tire is designed to cope with all off-road situations. The widely spaced lugs discharge mud and small stones easily, while the horizontal central bands provide much-needed traction during acceleration.

Presta valve   Schraeder valve

VALVES

Loosen the barrel on a Presta valve to inflate the tube. A car pump can be used to inflate a tube with a Schraeder valve.

TUBES

In addition to the conventional butyl rubber tube shown here, other types of tubes are available. So-called "puncture-proof" tubes are filled with a synthetic liquid sealant, and although this tends to make them heavy and harsh to ride, they can be useful for commuting. Latex tubes are very light and are widely used in racing. Despite their light weight, their elasticity makes them surprisingly puncture-resistant.

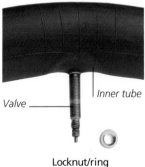

Inner tube

Valve

Locknut/ring

Dust cap

TWO-MINUTE TUBE CHANGE

1 REMOVE THE VALVE

Undo the valve dust cap and locknut. On the Presta valve, undo the valve and push it in to completely deflate the tube. On a Schraeder valve, use a pen, screwdriver, or other small implement to push in the valve. Press the valve stem through the hole in the rim.

Valve

Tire bead

Rim well

2 FREE THE TIRE

Pinch the tire walls firmly together all the way around the tire, pushing them back and forth to work the tire bead away from the rim. The tire and rim should then separate easily. Make sure the beads on each side are down in the rim well. If necessary, raise the tube valve clear of the bead.

3 UNHOOK THE TIRE

If the tire is a loose fit, it should be possible to lift one side over the rim with your hands. If the tire is tight, carefully insert a tire lever, making sure not to pinch the tube, and lever the tire bead over the rim. Work all around the rim until one wall of the tire is completely off the rim.

Tire lever

4 REMOVE THE INNER TUBE

Lift the valve out through the valve hole, being careful not to damage the threads on the valve body. Remove the tube from the tire. If you need to repair a puncture, follow the instructions on p.37. If you are replacing the tube with a new one, check that it is clean, dry, and the correct size.

5 CHECK THE TIRE

Feel along the inside and outside of the tire with your fingers. Remove any embedded foreign bodies before inserting a new or repaired tube. If the tube is punctured on the rim side, the cause may be a protruding spoke. If you cannot file the spoke down, cover it with several layers of tape. Turn the page for Step 6.

TUBE CHANGE continued

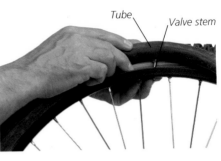
Tube
Valve stem

6 REPLACE THE TUBE

Partially inflate the replacement or repaired tube. This makes the tube easier to work with, as it has enough shape to avoid being creased, wrinkled, or pinched when you replace the tire. Place the tube inside the tire and insert the valve stem through the valve hole in the rim, making sure it is straight. Then thread the valve locknut or ring loosely onto the stem.

Tire bead

7 REPLACE THE TIRE

Tuck the rest of the tube carefully into the tire, ensuring it is evenly spread all the way around the inside of the tire, then deflate it completely. Push the valve stem up into the tire as far as the locknut. Slip the tire bead over the rim. Keep the valve stem clear of the rim or the bead may catch on it, creating a bulge in the tire that may damage the tube.

8 SECURE THE TIRE

Press the side of the tire over the rim with your thumbs. Work back and forth rhythmically to keep the tire from popping off at either side. Knead the tire with a steady pressure; if you feel it getting very tight, reach across it and yank it firmly into place. Check that the tube has not been pinched between the rim and the tire, then reinflate it fully.

TUBULAR TIRES

To save weight and maintain high pressure, professional racing cyclists often use tubular tires ("tubs"), which are tube and tire in one. The tire casings are sewn together with the tube inside, and the tire is then glued to the rim. The casings are made of cotton or silk, and the tread vulcanized (heat-treated) either by machine or hand. Riders then have to let the tires dry out to the right consistency: too moist and they may pick up grit and puncture; too dry and the tire may slip. However, advances in conventional tire design have made tubs a rarity on racing bikes.

REPAIRING A PUNCTURE

You need a repair kit with patches and a tube of rubber cement; sandpaper and chalk are also recommended. The key to a successful repair is thorough preparation and cleanliness. If your hands get dirty when you remove the wheel, clean them so that no oil gets on the inner tube. To locate the puncture, inflate the tube and hold it next to your face, and rotate it. If you cannot feel or hear any air escaping, test the valve with a drop of spit. If you still cannot trace the hole, fully inflate the tube, immerse it in water, and watch for air bubbles.

Rubber cement

Rectangular repair patch

Round repair patches

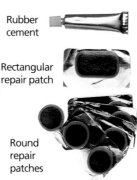

1 PREPARE THE TUBE

Once you have found the puncture, dry the tube and roughen the area around the puncture with sandpaper. This helps the rubber cement adhere to the surface. Make the sanded area larger than the repair patch. If you do not have any sandpaper, a coarse, flat stone surface will do, such as concrete. Give the tube one last thorough cleaning.

2 APPLY THE CEMENT

Clean your hands. Spread an even layer of rubber cement over the sanded area. Let the cement dry until tacky, so that the solvent in the cement evaporates. Do not allow anything to touch the cement during this time. With the tube in a safe place, check the tire for damage while you wait (see Step 5, p.35).

3 PATCH THE PUNCTURE

Peel off the foil on the patch, being careful not to touch the adhesive area that you expose. Press the patch firmly and centrally down over the puncture hole, rubbing from the center to the edges. Use sandpaper to powder the chalk, sprinkling it over any excess cement around the patch.

4 FINAL CHECK

Leave the patch to set for one or two minutes, then pinch the tube and patch together so that the cellophane backing of the patch splits. Peel the cellophane away from the center without peeling off the patch. Inflate the tube and check the patch. Replace the tube and the tire (see p.36).

Transmission

THE TERM TRANSMISSION IS USED to describe those mechanical parts of a bike that work in unison to transmit the cyclist's pedaling power to the bike's wheels by means of a system of gears. Transmission systems typically include a shift lever, cables, and the gear changing mechanism, of which there are two kinds: internal rear hub changer (most famous being the long-lived, three-speed Sturmey Archer model used on utility bikes), and those featuring front and rear derailleurs, standard issue on mountain and road bikes. Almost all bikes today are equipped with a gear changing mechanism, except track-racing bikes and some time-trial bikes, which have a single chainring and one fixed (non-freewheeling) cog on the rear wheel; the cranks do not stop rotating when the rider stops pedaling, so the rider has to keep moving with the pedals until the bike comes to a halt.

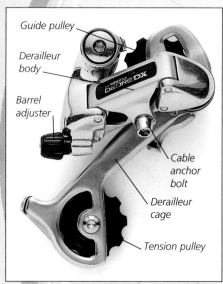

Guide pulley

Derailleur body

Barrel adjuster

SHIMANO DEORE DX

Cable anchor bolt

Derailleur cage

Tension pulley

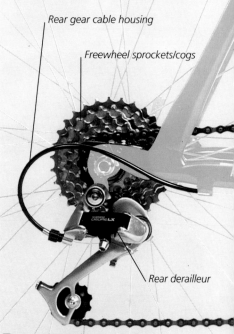

Rear gear cable housing

Freewheel sprockets/cogs

SHIMANO DEORE LX

Rear derailleur

REAR DERAILLEUR

As the chain comes off the bottom of a front chainring it passes through the rear derailleur on jockey wheels (the tension pulley and guide pulley). The cage holding the wheels is fixed to the main body of the changer by a pivot and is held under constant spring tension to keep the chain taut. The side-to-side travel of the derailleur cage is limited by adjustable screws.

FREEWHEEL

Freewheels divide into two categories: those that are part of the wheel hub, and others that are cassettes that slide or thread onto the hub. The freewheel has a central body onto which the cogs are threaded, or slide on splines (slots).

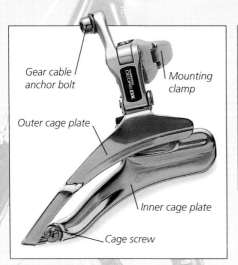

Gear cable anchor bolt

Mounting clamp

Outer cage plate

Inner cage plate

Cage screw

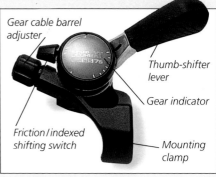

Gear cable barrel adjuster

Thumb-shifter lever

Gear indicator

Friction / indexed shifting switch

Mounting clamp

FRONT DERAILLEUR

This consists of a metal cage through which the chain passes as it feeds onto the front chainrings. The cage moves from side to side, and pressing on the side of the chain shifts it between the chainrings. The derailleur uses a pivot system to keep the sides of the cage vertical.

THUMB-SHIFTER

Shift levers can be mounted on the down tube, the top tube, the stem, or on the handlebars. (Thumb-shifters are for handlebars only.) Cables lead from the shifters to the derailleurs, and when activated, the derailleurs move laterally, guiding the chain between freewheel sprockets or chainrings. Some modern shifters have double levers for pushing with the thumb and pulling with the forefinger.

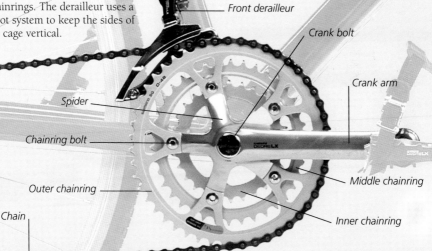

Front derailleur

Crank bolt

Crank arm

Spider

Chainring bolt

Middle chainring

Outer chainring

Inner chainring

Chain

CHAIN

The chain should be the correct width to operate smoothly over the sprockets and chainrings, and the correct length for optimum shifting performance. Grit builds up on chains fast, so they need regular cleaning.

CRANKS AND CHAINRINGS

In contrast to the freewheel sprockets, the larger the chainring the higher the gear. Most bikes today have a series of chainrings to give a wide range of gear ratios. Cranks range in length from 165–180 mm, with 170 mm average for mountain bikes, and 175 mm average for road bikes.

Chains

CLEAN, WELL-LUBRICATED CHAINS can be up to 98 percent efficient (see p.71–72). Dirt causes link rivets to enlarge the holes in the link plates; the chain stretches and ceases to mesh smoothly with the teeth on the chainrings and sprockets. Derailleur shifting suffers, and under pressure the chain will jump. When replacing a chain, also change the chainrings and sprockets: a new chain will kick on worn sprockets. Be sure the new chain is the correct type for your transmission. Seek advice, because the quality of components can vary.

ANATOMY

Chain

Bushing

Inner link plate
Rivet head
Outer link plate

Sedis 2.38 mm standard chain

Sedis 2.38 mm gold chain

Shimano HyperGlide chain

CHAIN TYPES
Various chains have been developed for different bicycle types and uses. Five- or six-speed bicycles will have a wider chain than a seven- or eight-speed. Older, non-derailleur chains are broken at a master link, whereas the more modern type can be broken at any point along their length, using a chain tool.

BROKEN CHAINS
Exerting too much pressure on an older chain can cause one of the links to break. To repair it you must have a chain tool or rivet extractor, so always keep one in your basic tool kit (see pp.16–17). Chains, especially those on mountain bikes, take a lot of punishment. If your chain needs frequent repair, replace it.

CHECK FOR WEAR
Test the chain for wear by lifting it up when it is on the large chainring. If one of the chainwheel teeth is fully exposed beneath it, the chain is worn out. Replace the chain, the chainrings, and the sprockets at the same time if they are worn and you can afford to; a new chain will perform badly on worn sprockets.

DISMANTLING AND REASSEMBLY

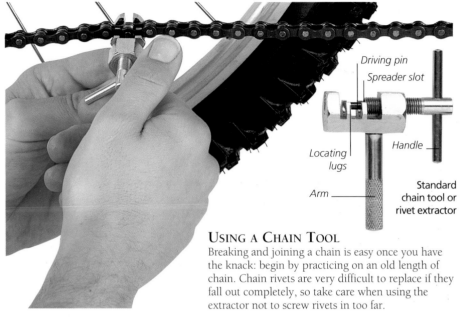

Driving pin

Spreader slot

Locating lugs

Handle

Arm

Standard chain tool or rivet extractor

USING A CHAIN TOOL

Breaking and joining a chain is easy once you have the knack: begin by practicing on an old length of chain. Chain rivets are very difficult to replace if they fall out completely, so take care when using the extractor not to screw rivets in too far.

1 POSITION THE CHAIN

Nest the chain in the chain tool by laying the chain flat, and slotting it firmly between the locating lugs. Then make sure the outer link plate is braced against the back of the tool. Do this by centering the driving pin exactly against the chain rivet, ensuring the chain stays in place, and slowly tightening the handle.

2 DISPLACE THE RIVET

To displace the rivet, rotate the chain tool handle 6 to 6½ turns until the rivet is clear of the inner link plate but is still just held in place by the outer link plate. Standard extractor tools like the one shown here have an open back. More expensive models have an adjustable screw that keeps the rivets being from driven out too far. They may also have a longer handle arm for increased leverage. Turn the page for Step 3.

Rivet

Inner link plate

DISMANTLING AND REASSEMBLY continued

3 SEPARATE THE LINKS
Flex the chain to separate the link from its neighbor. If the rivet has not been driven out far enough, you may have to use the chain tool again to drive the rivet a little farther out. Work with care, turning the handle slowly. Only rotate by ⅓ turn at a time, so that the rivet does not pop out of the outer link plate.

Bushing

Rivet

Driving pin

Rivet

4 REPLACE THE RIVET
To rejoin the links, position the chain in the tool (see Step 1, p.41), with the protruding rivet against the driving pin. Firmly tighten the handle to drive the rivet in, but if it sticks, back the driving pin off, wiggle the link to line up the rivet with the holes, and try again. Using excessive force may distort the chain or the rivet, which will result in chain malfunction.

5 POSITION THE RIVET
Stop driving the rivet in when it just juts out of the outer link plate. The rivet should also be jutting slightly out of the link plate nearest the driving pin, since the process will have compressed the components together.

Outer link plate

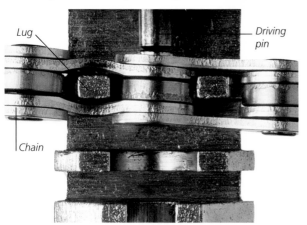

Lug

Driving pin

Chain

6 FLEX THE LINK
Nest the chain firmly in the spreader slot (the space between the pair of lugs nearest to the tool handle) with the driving pin against the most prominent end of the rivet. Gently – ⅓ turn or so should be sufficient – tighten the handle to move the rivet slightly farther and open up the link. This process ensures that there is just enough required flexibility between the inner plate, the outer plate, and the bushing.

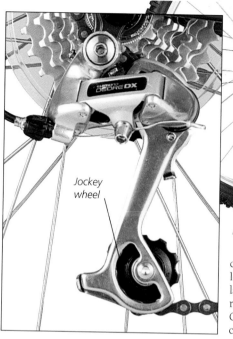

Jockey wheel

7 CORRECT THE CHAIN LENGTH

A new chain will not necessarily be the correct length for your transmission. Set the length of a new chain so that when it is on the largest chainring and smallest sprocket, the rear-derailleur jockey wheels align vertically. Check that the chain remains taut when the chain is on the smallest chainring and sprocket.

NON-DERAILLEUR ⅛-INCH CHAIN

This type of chain is joined by a master link. It is dismantled simply by removing the spring clip and the end plate, then pulling the link out. When replaced, the spring clip's closed end should face the direction of travel.

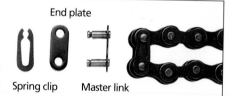

End plate

Spring clip

Master link

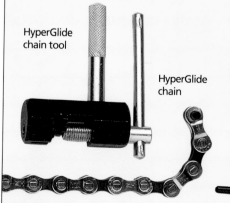

HyperGlide chain tool

HyperGlide chain

SPECIAL CHAINS AND TOOLS

Bicycles equipped with Shimano groupsets are usually fitted with a HyperGlide chain. Rivets are replaceable, but a special chain tool is required.

CONNECTING RIVET

HyperGlide chains should not be broken twice in the same place. Drive in the pointed end of the new rivet with the tool, then break off the excess with pliers.

HyperGlide chain rivet

Cables

TRANSMISSION CABLES COME IN different lengths
and thicknesses, and with different types of
nipples. Always use the right size and type of
cable, particularly for gear changing systems.
Either order for your make and model of bike,
or take the bike or old cables to a shop. Keep a
spare set in case one breaks. Transmission cables
must be good quality, especially for indexed
gearing systems, since the movement at the lever
must be precisely reproduced at the derailleur.
If the cable wire or housing flexes or compresses,
accurate gear changing is impossible.

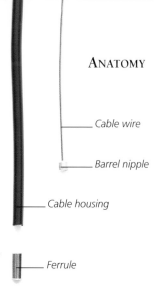

ANATOMY

Cable wire

Barrel nipple

Cable housing

Ferrule

CABLE GUIDES

Slotted cable guides (left) are fitted to some
frames. These allow the cable wires to be
regreased by sliding sections of housing
along the wire, thereby dispensing with
the need to remove the
cable completely and
disturb the gear
indexing.

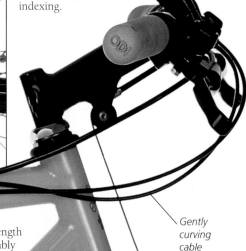

Gently
curving
cable

CABLE HOUSING

Replace damaged cable housing and frayed
cables as soon as possible. Cut housing to a length
that gives a gentle curve between guides, notably
between the handlebars and frame: this allows
the wire inside to operate smoothly. If, after
cutting cable housing, the ends are burred
or uneven, neaten them with a file.

REPLACING TRANSMISSION CABLES

1 UNTHREAD CABLE

Undo the derailleur cable anchor bolt. Dismantle the shifter by removing the shift lever from its mounting plate or clamp. Pull out the old cable wire. Grease and thread the new wire. Reassemble the shifter. (Some shifters are so designed that they do not need dismantling; simply remove the barrel adjuster, then thread the new cable throught the unit.) Be sure cable housing is snug in barrel adjusters and guides.

2 ATTACH CABLE

With the chain on the smallest chainring and sprocket, pass the cable through the derailleur anchor bolt. Tug the cable firmly and tighten the bolt. Pull on an exposed length of wire to stretch it. Take up any slack by redoing the anchor bolt. Adjust the gears (see pp.46–51). (Note that if you are replacing the rear derailleur cable, be sure to reverse the barrel adjuster on the derailleur two turns to allow for fine-tuning later.)

RECENT SHIFTER DESIGNS

Shimano's Rapid Fire and its successor, Rapid Fire Plus, are the latest in shifter design. Rapid Fire uses the thumb to operate both up- and down-shift levers. Rapid Fire Plus shifts the chain down a gear by pushing a thumb lever forward, and up a gear by pulling a separate lever back with the forefinger.

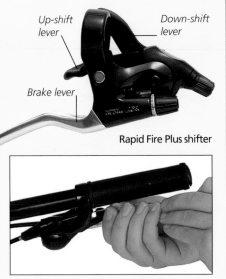

Up-shift lever

Down-shift lever

Brake lever

Rapid Fire Plus shifter

RAPID FIRE CABLE RENEWAL

Changing the cable wire is a relatively simple operation on Rapid Fire systems. Once disconnected at the derailleur, the cable wire can be pulled out of the access hole in the shifter body. Replacement is simply a case of threading the wire back down the hole. On Rapid Fire shifters, the outer casing has to be removed first.

Rear Derailleur

AS THE RIDER CHANGES GEARS, the rear derailleur moves the chain to a selected cog, aligning the chain so it runs smoothly. Early derailleurs were controlled using simple, friction-tensioned levers that the rider had to position manually. Many systems still include a friction shifting option, but indexed and push-button shifting are now the norm. Modern derailleurs are easy to use but must be accurately adjusted. Side-to-side travel (movement) must be limited to stop the chain from jumping off the inner and outermost cogs.

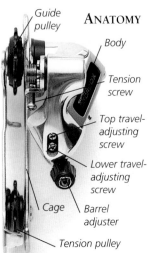

ANATOMY

Guide pulley

Body

Tension screw

Top travel-adjusting screw

Lower travel-adjusting screw

Cage

Barrel adjuster

Tension pulley

REAR DERAILLEUR TRAVEL ADJUSTMENT

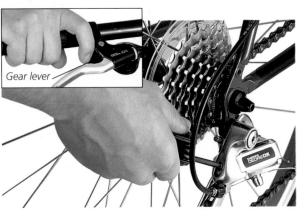

Gear lever

1 LIMIT TRAVEL IN TOP GEAR

With the bike on a workstand or similar support, pull the rear gear lever to shift the chain onto the smallest cog and the outer chainring (top gear). Slacken the top travel-adjusting screw until no resistance is felt. Screw it back in clockwise until both jockey wheels on the derailleur align with the small sprocket when viewed directly from behind.

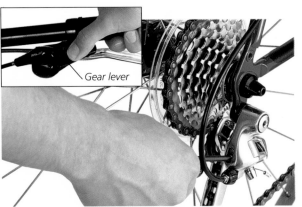

Gear lever

2 LIMIT TRAVEL IN BOTTOM GEAR

Push the rear gear lever with your thumb to shift the chain onto the largest sprocket and smallest chainring (bottom gear). Slacken the lower travel-adjusting screw until no resistance is felt. Now the jockey wheels will probably be slightly too close to the wheel spokes. Retighten the adjusting screw until the jockey wheels and the sprocket align.

Tension
screw

3 ADJUST TENSION SCREW

Run the chain onto the largest chainring and the smallest sprocket. Rotate the cranks and adjust the tension screw so that the guide pulley is as close to the smallest sprocket as possible, but not actually touching it. Turning the cranks again, run the chain onto the smallest chainring and the largest sprocket, checking that the guide pulley does not touch any of the sprockets. Adjust again if necessary.

REAR DERAILLEUR MOUNTING

For modern rear derailleurs to work well, the rear dropouts must be aligned with each other, and the derailleur hanger must be parallel with the center line of the bike. Frame alignment requires specific equipment and a high degree of skill, so should be done by a bike shop. As a rough test, stand behind the bike and visually check that a line through the guide and tension pulleys is parallel with (in the same plane as) the rear wheel. Derailleurs are often damaged in a crash or if the bike is dropped (see p.87).

REAR DERAILLEUR SERVICING

Undo the mounting bolt after removing the cable at the anchor bolt, and if the chain is on the bike, remove the tension and guide pulleys. To dismantle the cage (which is rarely needed), undo the cage stop screw (which prevents the cage from unwinding) and unwind it. Make a careful note of how many times it rotates, and, when you separate the cage and arm, the position of the spring. The spring tension on most derailleurs can be adjusted by placing the end of the spring in one of a series of holes inside the derailleur body. Lubricate the pivot pins on the body, then clean and lubricate the guide and tension pulleys with a light, fast grease (see pp.72–73).

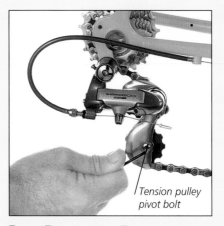

Tension pulley
pivot bolt

REAR DERAILLEUR REMOVAL

To remove the mechanism without breaking the chain, remove the tension pulley by undoing its mounting bolt with an Allen key. The guide pulley may also need loosening.

INDEXED GEAR SHIFTING ADJUSTMENT

Rear gear cable

Rear shifter

Barrel adjuster

1 PREPARE THE BIKE
Mount the bike on a workstand or other device to raise the rear wheel off the ground. With the chain on the middle chainring, use the rear shifter to shift the chain onto the smallest sprocket. Slacken the rear gear cable by turning the barrel adjuster on the rear derailleur all the way clockwise. Repeat with the barrel adjuster on the rear shifter, but this time finish off by reversing two turns to allow for fine-tuning later.

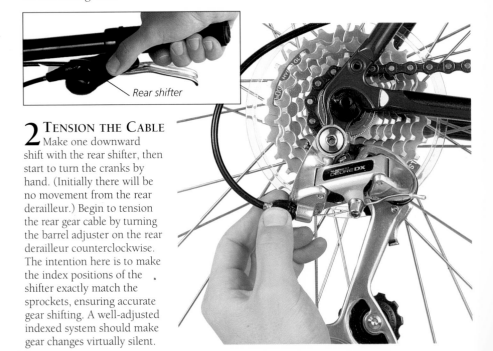

Rear shifter

2 TENSION THE CABLE
Make one downward shift with the rear shifter, then start to turn the cranks by hand. (Initially there will be no movement from the rear derailleur.) Begin to tension the rear gear cable by turning the barrel adjuster on the rear derailleur counterclockwise. The intention here is to make the index positions of the shifter exactly match the sprockets, ensuring accurate gear shifting. A well-adjusted indexed system should make gear changes virtually silent.

Barrel
adjuster

Derailleur
cage

3 FINAL CHECK

Continue reversing the barrel adjuster while turning the cranks, until the chain finally shifts up onto the second cog (thereby matching the position of the shifter). Continue turning the adjuster until the chain begins to catch on the third sprocket, then reverse it – but only enough to stop this catching. Finally, check the shifting operation between all cogs. Fine-tune the barrel adjuster if necessary, to provide positive shifting throughout the gears.

Cage aligns with cog

THUMB-SHIFTERS

The oldest thumb-shifter gearing systems offered no indexed shifting, whereas the most modern systems are indexed only. Combined systems are a happy medium.

OLD VERSUS NEW

This older twin-function thumb-shifter design allows the rider to switch between indexed and friction shifting. This is useful if the indexing becomes faulty and for fine-tuning the derailleur's position while riding. More recent all-indexed designs offer slicker shifting and greater comfort, but cannot match the reliability of their predecessors.

Switch for changing
from indexed to
friction shifting

Thumb-
shifter lever

Gear cable
barrel adjuster

Front Derailleur

THE FRONT DERAILLEUR SHIFTS the chain between the chainrings. Adjustments should be made to it when shifting between chainrings becomes inaccurate or noisy, and whenever the rear derailleur is adjusted; both derailleurs have to work together for the transmission to be effective. So, if you adjust the front derailleur while the chain is on the smallest chainring, the chain should be in line at the rear (that is, on the largest sprocket), and when on the outer chainring, on the smallest sprocket. Adjusting the derailleur is also an operational matter, meaning that after basic adjustments have been made with the bike on a workstand, you may need to fine-tune while you are actually riding.

ANATOMY

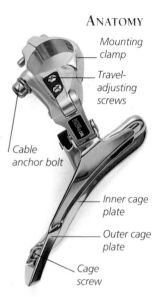

Mounting clamp

Travel-adjusting screws

Cable anchor bolt

Inner cage plate

Outer cage plate

Cage screw

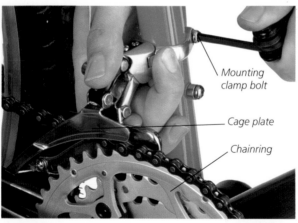

Mounting clamp bolt

Cage plate

Chainring

POSITIONING THE FRONT DERAILLEUR

The inner and outer derailleur cage plates must be parallel with the chainrings when viewed from above. Undo the mounting clamp bolt, then carefully position the mechanism. Tighten the clamp, and again check the plates against the chainrings. If they are parallel, finally tighten the clamp firmly, to avoid slipping, since the mechanism is under constant pressure from the shifter cable.

CHECKING FOR CLEARANCE

With the cage over the large chainring, use the mounting bolt to position the outer cage plate $\frac{1}{16}$–$\frac{1}{8}$ in (1.5–3 mm) above the chainring. A tighter clearance is needed for the closely spaced double chainrings, and a wider clearance for the broadly spaced triple chainrings. If your bike is fitted with elliptical Biopace rings, make adjustments with the crank pointed down in line with the seat tube, so that the highest part of the chainring is next to the cage plates.

FRONT DERAILLEUR TRAVEL ADJUSTMENT

1 LIMIT LEFT-HAND TRAVEL

Run the chain onto the small chainring and large sprocket. With triple chainrings, use the lower travel-adjust screw to set a clearance of ½₄–¹⁄₁₆ in (1–1.5 mm) between the inner cage plate and chain. With double chainrings, position the inner cage plate as close as possible to the chain without touching it. Test cable for slack. Tighten cable anchor bolt if needed.

2 LIMIT RIGHT-HAND TRAVEL

Run the chain to the large chainring and small sprocket. With the top travel-adjust screw, set the outer cage plate very close to, but not touching, the chain. On Shimano STI systems, run the chain to the middle chainring and large cog. Use the barrel adjuster on the shift lever to position the inner cage plate close to the chain.

DERAILLEUR/CRANK CLEARANCE

After correctly adjusting the front derailleur, the crank may just clip the outer cage plate when the chain is on the large chainring. If so, gently bend the outer plate inward with pliers, but not too far; the cage and chainring still have to align.

FRONT DERAILLEUR OPTIONS

Apart from standard bottom-pull mechanisms operated by wires threaded underneath the bottom bracket, other front derailleur system options include:

• Top-pull derailleur: in this design, the derailleur arm is pulled up from above, with the cable routed along the top tube and down the seat tube (as featured in the steps above). The benefit of this system is that the cable does not get clogged with mud, the major disadvantage of cables threaded underneath the bottom bracket.

• Bottom-pull derailleur adapted to top-pull set-up: this is done by threading the cable wire through a cable guide fixed to the derailleur arm, and allowing the cable housing to butt up against the guide. The wire is then anchored by a bolt fixed to the

seat tube above the bottom bracket (as shown above). This causes the standard cable operation to be reversed, so that when the shifter is activated, the cable housing actually slides over the wire (which remains static), forcing the derailleur arm to move.

Chainset

THE CHAINSET COMPRISES the chainrings and the cranks. Periodically check the chainring teeth for damage by removing the chain, placing a light behind the chainring, and rotating. Chipped teeth will be visible from the side, bent teeth from above. Also check that the chainrings are true. They can be bent into shape with a large wrench, but it is best to get this done at a bike shop. Regularly ensure that the crank bolts are snug (see below). Check the tightness of new cranks every 25 miles (40 km) for the first 200 miles (320 km) of use. See pp.62–63 for crank removal.

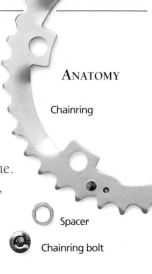

ANATOMY

Chainring

Spacer

Chainring bolt

TIGHTENING CRANKS

Remove dust caps and tighten the crank bolts with a wrench or crank tool. Tighten them firmly, but not too hard, in case the threads strip. If the bolts are alloy, first use a steel bolt to tighten the cranks, then replace the alloy bolts.

Crank mounting bolt socket

Crank

Spider arm

Crank arm

Threaded socket for pedal

CHECKING CRANKS

Creaking noises when riding are often caused by loose cranks. To test the cranks, position them horizontally, then press down hard on both pedals at once with your hands. Rotate the cranks 180°, then press down on the pedals again. If either crank moves, the crank mounting bolts need to be tightened.

TIGHTENING CHAINRINGS

1 CHECK THE CHAINRING BOLTS

Regularly check the tightness of the chainring bolts. Use the correct size of Allen key – usually 5 mm on most two- and three-ringed units. If the bolts are slack, tighten them.

2 TIGHTEN THE BOLTS

Move around the outer ring, tightening each bolt with equal pressure. Do not overtighten them, just take up any slack. Once they have been tightened a few times and have bedded in, secure them with a thread adhesive.

Chainring bolt

MOUNTAIN BIKE CHAINRINGS

The introduction of the mountain bike and its use on a variety of steep terrains, has necessitated the introduction of widely spaced gear ratios. This has affected chainwheel design and led to some problems with gear changing.

Special chain guides assist smooth gear changing

GEAR CHANGING PROBLEMS

Mountain bikes use chainring sets (above) with large differences in diameter, allowing a wide range of gear ratios. This set-up requires long chains and derailleur cages, which in turn can make gear changing in either direction slower and not as smooth as on a standard set-up.

Crank arm

MODIFIED DESIGN

Some manufacturers have developed new ways to improve gear changing. Shimano's HyperDrive chainrings (left) have a series of shorter (drop) teeth on the two outer rings to allow the chain to drop smoothly, and extra guide teeth on their sides to help pull the chain up.

Drop tooth

Freewheel and Sprockets

A FREEWHEEL IS FORMED of two main parts, one inside the other. The inner part threads or slides onto the hub. The outer body holds the various gear cogs, or sprockets. The inside of a freewheel is an intricate maze of small ratchet pawls, ball bearings, springs, and pins. It is important to keep it clean and lubricated (see pp.71–72), so that the pawls do not become clogged and stuck. Keep one ear tuned to your freewheel; if the steady whirring sound becomes at all ragged or uneven, then you will need to service or replace the freewheel as soon as possible.

Lockring

Sprocket
cluster

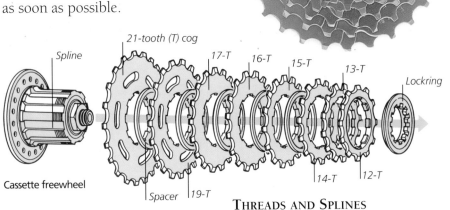

Spline

21-tooth (T) cog

17-T

16-T

15-T

13-T

Lockring

Cassette freewheel

Spacer   19-T

14-T   12-T

THREADS AND SPLINES

Freewheels divide into two main types. The threaded variety screws onto the hub complete with the cogs. The cassette freewheel is attached to the hub with the cogs sliding onto splines (slots) on its back; a lockring secures them in place.

Damaged
tooth

Broken teeth

BROKEN SPROCKET TEETH

Sprockets come under a great deal of force from the chain when the cyclist is pedaling up steep inclines. Sprocket teeth may eventually break as a result of this stress, and once one breaks, the remaining teeth are put under even more pressure. Change one or all worn or damaged sprockets immediately.

FREEWHEEL REMOVAL

Freewheel remover

FREEWHEEL TOOLS

Differences in freewheel tool design depend on the type of freewheel. To service a freewheel, you will need tools specific to it and your hub. Ask at a bike shop which tools you need.

1 FIT THE FREEWHEEL REMOVER

Remove the wheel nuts. Fit the freewheel remover over the axle and replace wheel nut or quick-release just tight enough to hold the remover in place.

2 LOOSEN OFF

Place the remover in a vise. Turn wheel counterclockwise until the freewheel breaks free. Remove the axle nut and spin the remover and freewheel off the hub. Grease the hub threads when refitting the freewheel.

Remover

Vise

Low ratio

High ratio

GEAR RATIOS

A gear, like a lever, is a means to change the rate at which work is done. The rate of change is called the ratio. On a bike the ratio is determined by the relative sizes of the crankset chainrings and the freewheel sprockets. With a 52-tooth (T) chainring, one complete turn of the cranks will rotate a wheel with a 13-T sprocket four times, a ratio of 4 to 1 (4:1). A 28-T chainring will turn a wheel with a 28-T sprocket once, a ratio of 1:1. A 52/13-T gear is big, and gives speed, while a 28/28-T gear is low, and gives the power to climb hills, albeit slowly.

Alternative Transmission Systems

THE MOST POPULAR ALTERNATIVE to the derailleur transmission system is the internal rear hub mechanism, which has a range of two, three, five and seven speeds. To change gear, a shift lever on the handlebars activates, via a cable, a control rod that passes through the hollow rear hub spindle. The mechanism needs little maintenance, apart from occasional lubrication and cable adjustment. Alternatives to the traditional chain transmission include belt and treadle drives (see glossary).

ROADSTER BIKE
Most utility bicycles, such as the roadster bike shown here, have traditionally used internal rear hub gear systems. Although hub gears are mechanically sophisticated, they are extremely dependable, and simple to use and service. Derailleur systems provide greater performance efficiency, but need more frequent servicing.

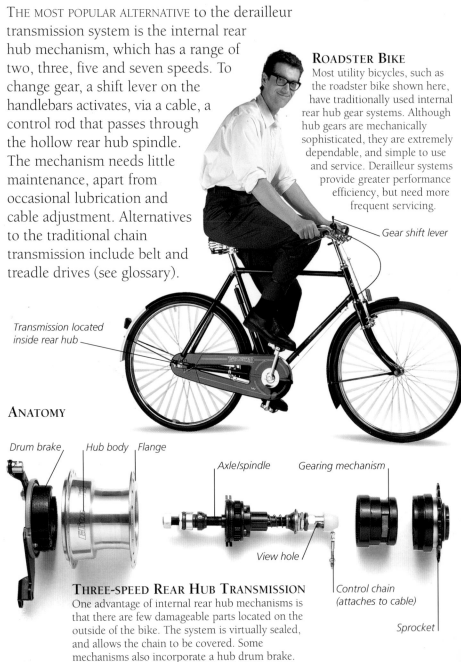

Gear shift lever

Transmission located inside rear hub

ANATOMY

Drum brake   Hub body   Flange

Axle/spindle   Gearing mechanism

View hole

Control chain
(attaches to cable)

Sprocket

THREE-SPEED REAR HUB TRANSMISSION
One advantage of internal rear hub mechanisms is that there are few damageable parts located on the outside of the bike. The system is virtually sealed, and allows the chain to be covered. Some mechanisms also incorporate a hub drum brake.

REAR HUB MECHANISM ADJUSTMENT (3-SPEED)

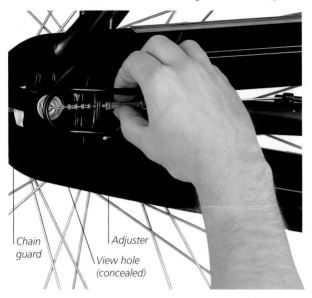

Chain guard

Adjuster

View hole (concealed)

1 CHECK CABLES
If there is any problem with the system, first check the cable and cable guides for stretching and damage, and adjust or replace as required.

2 LUBRICATE
If the mechanism has not been lubricated for some time, trickle drops of medium oil into it via the oiling nipple, and onto the control chain. Rotate cranks a few times in each gear.

3 ADJUST (3-SPEED)
Using the view hole, check the control rod and first link of the control chain exactly align when in second gear; if not, use the adjuster to align them.

LOOKING TO THE FUTURE
Developments in transmission technology include a computerized system that automatically changes gears in response to changes in pressure on the pedals and pedaling speed, both of which are monitored by sensors in the hub. When a pre-set range is exceeded, an electronic mechanism slides the rear sprocket to a new position and a new gear ratio.

BELT DRIVES
The quest for a lighter, cleaner, quieter, and lubrication-free alternative to the bicycle chain has resulted in many experiments with notched rubber belt drives, as on the Twike (above). Belt drives are already used on some folding bicycles.

TREADLE DRIVES
Treadle drives could become popular with Human-Powered Vehicles (see glossary), since the driving motion is linear, not circular as with pedaling.

Bearings

ESSENTIALLY BEARINGS ACT as a support between two reciprocal mechanical parts (cup and cones) that rotate on each other. Made of stainless steel, bearings are precision-engineered to very accurate sizes. It is incredible how such small components can be so integrally important to the maximum efficiency of the bicycle. Indeed, bearings that are well greased and set for almost no resistance or play are vital to bike performance and speed. The ride and handling of a little-serviced bike improves dramatically once the main bearings (the headset and bottom bracket) and front and rear wheel hub bearings have been overhauled. Modern bearing components often feature sealed unit bearings for easy maintenance.

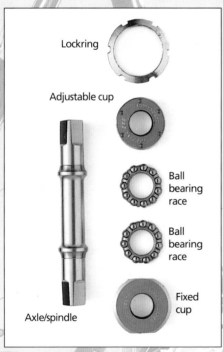

Lockring

Adjustable cup

Ball bearing race

Ball bearing race

Fixed cup

Axle/spindle

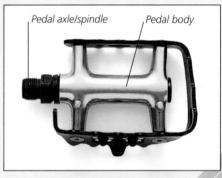

Pedal axle/spindle   Pedal body

PEDAL BEARINGS

It is vital to make sure your pedals are secure and the axles are straight. Also check and adjust your pedal bearings regularly for maximum energy efficiency. There are various types of pedals available, from traditional to step-in, or clipless, designs, which were originally developed from ski bindings.

BOTTOM BRACKET

To accommodate different frame and crank designs, bottom bracket axle lengths vary. Adjustable, cassette, and self-contained bottom bracket bearings need servicing more regularly if they are exposed to a lot of water, grit, and mud.

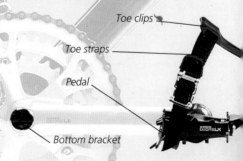

Toe clips

Toe straps

Pedal

Bottom bracket

Top headset
bearing assembly

Bottom headset
bearing assembly

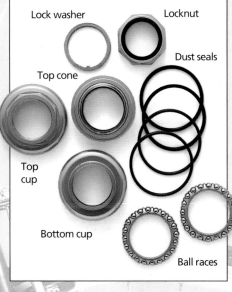

Lock washer

Locknut

Top cone

Dust seals

Top
cup

Bottom cup

Ball races

HEADSETS

Headset assemblies are engineered by bicycle
designers to endure a great amount of impact.
Some modern designs incorporate roller
bearings, which are cylindrical rather than
spherical (ball) bearings, their advantage being
that load is distributed over a greater surface
area. However, most headsets still use
conventional ball bearings, as they are far
more economical to manufacture.

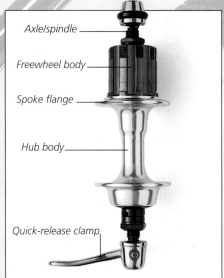

Axle/spindle

Freewheel body

Spoke flange

Hub body

Quick-release clamp

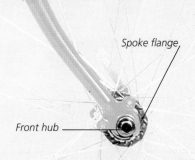

Spoke flange

Front hub

WHEEL HUBS

The shape of wheel hubs varies to some
extent between manufacturers, but the
basic components are the same. Hubs are
available with adjustable bearings or
replaceable cassette bearings, which are
precision-machined for smoothness.

Headset

THE HEADSET HOLDS THE forks (steerer tube) in
the head tube. Test for faults by lifting the
front wheel off the ground and rotating the
handlebars with one finger. They should move
smoothly; if there are any grinding noises or
the forks catch in certain positions, then the
bearings need adjustment or regreasing. You
should also test the headset for slack (below,
right). Loose bearings must be corrected
immediately, since stresses in the headset area
are high, and a loose headset can self-destruct
rapidly. You will need to use special headset
wrenches; 32 mm wrenches for most bikes;
36 mm for some mountain bikes. If the headset
parts are alloy, take care not to bend them.

ANATOMY

Top bearing set

— Locknut

— Locknut washer

— Adjustable top cup

— Dust seal

— Ball bearing race

— Fixed top cone

Bottom bearing set

— Fixed bottom cup

— Ball bearing race

— Dust seal

— Fixed bottom cone

Top bearing set

HIGH STRESS ZONE
The head tube and headset
have to tolerate a lot of
impact stress within a
relatively small area. It is
not uncommon for the
headset to work itself
loose, so regular
checks are advisable.

The head tube
houses the forks,
which in turn
house the
handlebar stem ⎯

Bottom
bearing
set ⎯

TESTING FOR SLACK
Firmly engage the front brake, then push the
bike back and forth. A *click-clunk* sound
indicates loose headset bearings or brake
mounting bolts. Lift and lightly rotate the
handlebars; roughness indicates too tight
bearings and/or that they need regreasing.

Headset Adjustment

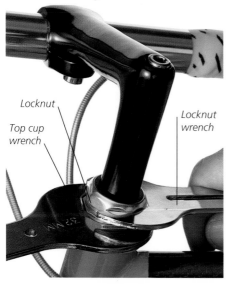

Locknut

Top cup
wrench

Locknut
wrench

1 Loosen Locknut
First make sure you have the correct headset wrenches; ill-fitting ones will damage the locknut and may distort the bearing surfaces. Loosen the locknut counterclockwise. (Locknuts with castellations rather than flat edges can also be carefully loosened with a small cold-chisel.) Now slacken off the top cup – you should be able to use your fingers.

2 Adjust and Tighten Top Cup
Gradually turn the top cup clockwise until it is finger-tight against the bearings and there is no play in the set. Reverse the cup ⅛–¼ turn, and hold it in position with one of the headset wrenches. Then, using the other wrench, lock the cup in place by carefully applying a medium amount of clockwise force on the locknut. Always work from an adjustment that is just loose enough to avoid overtightening the bearings when you secure the locknut.

Annual Rebuild
Headsets are exposed to stress, dirt, and road shocks, so they should be stripped, cleaned, and rebuilt at least once a year.

• Remove the handlebar stem (see p.15), then the locknut and washer. Secure the forks to the frame with string, or hold them in place with one hand.

• Remove the adjustable top cup. If the ball bearings are loose, most will stick to the inside of the cup, so count them out. If they are held in a race, simply lift it out. Slowly draw the forks out of the head tube. If the lower bearings are loose, gather them all together and count them.

• Clean all parts in a biodegradable solvent and wipe the fixed cones. Ball bearings must be smooth and unpitted. Cones and cups should be evenly colored where the balls run. Check the running grooves for brinneling (a series of small dents caused by very hard impacts).

• Place the ball races on a glass surface to see if they are bent or warped. If the headset needs replacing, get a bike shop to do it.

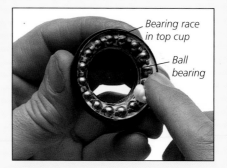

Bearing race
in top cup

Ball
bearing

• Wash your hands thoroughly. This keeps the grease you use from getting contaminated. Assuming all parts are in good condition, lightly line the inside of the adjustable top cup (pictured above) and fixed bottom cup with a stiff, waterproof grease.

• Position the ball bearings and press them right into the grease. Add sufficient grease to coat each bearing. Be careful – too much grease will leak, attract dirt, and create a mess.

• Replace the forks and all other parts carefully, so that no ball bearings dislodge. Finally adjust as in Step 2, above.

Bottom Bracket

THE BOTTOM BRACKET axle, or spindle, rotates on bearings inside the bottom bracket shell. There are two common basic types of bottom brackets: adjustable (using cups and cones threaded into the bracket shell) and sealed cassette (where axle and bearings are a complete unit held in place within the bracket shell). Some cassettes are adjustable; most are not. Bottom brackets with adjustable bearings usually have a fixed cup (with no lockring) on the right-hand side, and an adjustable cup with holes and a lockring on the left-hand side. The bottom bracket axle and bearings should be cleaned and regreased at least once a year.

ANATOMY

Lockring

Adjustable cup

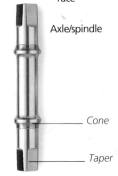
Ball bearing race

Axle/spindle

Cone

Taper

Ball bearing race

Fixed cup

BOTTOM BRACKET REMOVAL

1 REMOVE DUST CAP
To adjust the bottom bracket or strip it for cleaning and regreasing, the cranks must be removed. Take the dust caps off; if they have smooth surfaces, they are press-fitted and can be pried off. If the caps have Allen key bolts or slots, unscrew them with the appropriate tool.

Crank mounting bolt

2 REMOVE CRANK BOLT
Once the dust caps are off, undo and remove the crank mounting bolts using a wrench or crank extractor. Be sure no washers are left inside. When you come to replace the crank bolts, make sure they are snug, but not too tight, as the threads may strip. (Note that crank bolts on new bikes need to be checked for tightness regularly.)

3 REMOVE CRANK WITH EXTRACTOR

Turn the inside bolt on the crank extractor counterclockwise as far as it will go, then screw the extractor housing (which is threaded on the outside) firmly into the crank. Use a wrench if necessary. Turn the inside bolt clockwise until firm, but not too tight – if the crank is alloy, the threads may strip if forced. Remove the crank by tapping it with a wooden mallet. If it does not give, slowly increase the extractor tension, levering sharply when the crank starts to yield. Remove really stubborn cranks with a hammer and drift punch, or go to a bike shop.

4 TEST BEARINGS

Test bearings for excess play by pushing a crank to and fro firmly. A clicking sound indicates loose bearings. Lift the chain off the chainring and rest it on the bottom bracket. Spin the chainwheel; if it catches or runs roughly, the bearings are too tight and/or need regreasing.

5 ADJUST BEARINGS

Make sure the fixed cup on the chainwheel side is tight; remove the crank arm and spider to get at it. This cup has a left-hand thread and is tightened counterclockwise. On the chainless side, turn the adjustable cup finger-tight against the bearings, then reverse it by ⅛ turn or so. Check bearings for play; a little is needed to compensate for tightening the lockring. Tighten lockring firmly with a lockring or pin wrench.

BEARING CASSETTES

Sealed bottom bracket bearing cassettes are relatively inexpensive, maintenance-free disposable units. They will usually last up to two years under normal use, or about a year under heavy use.

CASSETTE REMOVER

The Shimano hexagonal removing tool shown here is specifically designed to extract Shimano bottom bracket bearing cassettes.

FAG-TYPE CASSETTE

Above is a typical example, made by FAG, of a disposable, nonadjustable sealed bottom bracket bearing cassette. The molded shell, which holds the internal metal components in place, is made from a durable nylon plastic. One end of the cassette is detachable, to allow for fitting.

Hubs

CONVENTIONAL HUB BEARINGS (those with adjustable cones that allow the bearings to be removed, tightened, or loosened) should be checked regularly, adjusted, and cleaned and lubricated if necessary, for maximum wheel performance. This should be at the point where there is no resistance to the hub's rotation or any excess play. Cleaning and lubrication should be done more often if you ride a lot in wet and muddy conditions. More up-to-date cassette hub bearings should also be removed and replaced when necessary, but they are fairly durable and can last up to two years or more.

ANATOMY

 Locknut

 Washer

 Adjustable cone

 Ball bearings

CHECKING FOR BINDING

Remove the wheel, hold it directly in front of you, and spin it. If you feel any sticking or roughness as the wheel rotates, the bearings are too tight (binding), and the cones need adjusting.

Hub body

Ball bearings

Axle/spindle

CHECK FOR EXCESS PLAY

With the wheel in the rear dropouts and the axle nuts snug (tightening the axle nuts or a quick-release slightly tightens the bearings), push the wheel to and fro. If you feel any clicking, the bearings are loose (excess play) and the cones need adjusting.

Axle nuts snug in rear dropouts

HUB SERVICE AND ADJUSTMENT

1 REMOVE FREEWHEEL
Both screw-on or Shimano HyperGlide (cassette unit) freewheels must be removed (see p.55) before the rear hub bearing cones can be adjusted.

2 DISMANTLE HUB
Remove the locknuts, washers, cones, and the axle. Count the ball bearings as you remove them. Clean all parts in solvent and dry. Pack the hub cups with grease and press the ball bearings right into it.

3 ADJUST CONE
On wheels with freehubs, first make sure the right-side locknut and cone are secure. Using a pair of cone wrenches, undo the left-side locknut and cone, taking care not to dislodge the bearings. Screw the cone tight against the bearings with your fingers, and reverse it by ⅛ turn or so. Now secure the cone with the locknut. Test again with the axle nuts or quick-release clamp in place. Readjust if necessary.

CASSETTE BEARINGS
Cassette, or cartridge, bearings are the service-free answer to hub bearings. They are sealed units made up of a cup, a cone, ball bearings, and grease. When play develops or the bearings are worn, the cartridges need replacing. Undo the grubscrews to remove the spacers and the axle. Then tap the cartridges out. Use thread adhesive to fix new cassettes in place, then replace the spacers and tighten the grubscrews.

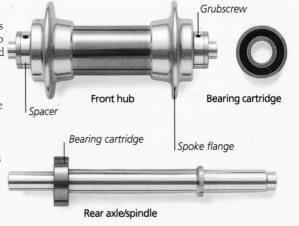

Grubscrew

Spacer

Front hub

Bearing cartridge

Bearing cartridge

Spoke flange

Rear axle/spindle

Pedals

PEDALS CAN BE FITTED with either loose ball bearings held in place by an adjustable cone, or a self-contained cassette press-fitted into the pedal body. Some cassette bearings can be adjusted, others cannot. They can last for over two years or more without servicing, but if you do decide to service them you will need specialized tools. Many people do not bother; when their old pedals start creaking and grinding, they replace rather than repair them. Pedals with adjustable bearings should be cleaned and regreased every six months. The longevity of pedals depends on their quality; good ones will naturally last longer.

ANATOMY

Dust cap

Locknut

Washer

Adjustable cone

Ball bearings

Toe straps

Toe clips

Crank

CHECKING A PEDAL

To check the pedal bearings, grasp the pedal with one hand and the crank with the other, then push the pedal back and forth. Clicking sounds indicate the bearings are loose. Spin the pedals. Any grinding and sticking means the bearings are too tight. If you use toe clips, check them for splits or cracks. Check that straps are in good condition, and that the buckles do not slip.

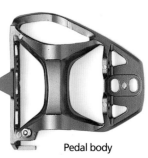

Pedal body

Ball bearings

REMOVING PEDALS

Remove both pedals from the cranks with a thin-jawed wrench, or, if the pedal axle threads are well greased, by unscrewing the sockets on the crank ends of the pedal axles with an Allen key. Remember the left-side pedal has a left-hand thread and should be unscrewed clockwise. Right-side pedals have normal right-hand threads and should be unscrewed counterclockwise.

Left-side pedal axle thread

MS-L

Axle/spindle

Fixed cone

Axle thread

SERVICING A PEDAL

1 REMOVE DUST CAP

The purpose of dust caps is to protect the pedal bearings from water and dirt. Remove the dust cap to gain access to the locknut. Alloy dust caps are threaded, so unscrew them with an adjustable wrench or use a special tool if the dust cap is unique. Sometimes plastic dust caps are threaded as well, so try unscrewing them first. If that does not work, pry the dust cap off with a thin screwdriver.

Dust cap

Axle

Wrench

Locknut

2 DISMANTLE THE PEDAL

Hold the crank end of the pedal axle with a wrench, and unscrew the locknut and the adjustable cone. Shake out and count the ball bearings. Remove the axle, and shake out and count the ball bearings from the crank end. Clean all parts. Regrease the cups and press the ball bearings right into the grease. Replace the axle, and screw the cone in finger-tight. Replace the washer and the locknut. Spin the pedal to nest the bearings in place. Turn the cone flush against the bearings, then reverse it by ⅛ turn or so. Tighten the locknut, and check adjustment. Replace the dust cap, grease the axle threads, and reinstall the pedal.

STEP-IN SYSTEM PEDALS

Step-in, or clipless, pedals work together with compatible cleats. When the rider steps onto the pedal, a mechanism automatically grips on the cleat. The tension in this mechanism can be adjusted by a bolt located behind or underneath the pedal.

Adjustable cleat-grip mechanism

Spindle nut

Cartridge bearing

Cleat tension bolts

OFF-ROAD PEDALS

Double-sided pedals like the Shimano SPD (right) are specially designed for off-road use. Compatible shoes have recessed clips, so the rider can walk or run freely if necessary.

COMPONENTS

Step-in pedal axles use sealed cartridge bearings. If a pedal rattles, the spindle nut or bearing cartridge may be loose.

Routine Maintenance

BIKES ARE MACHINES, AND PERFORM best when well tuned and looked after. Every rider can provide this for his or her bike by way of routine maintenance, which includes keeping the bike clean, lubricated, and regularly serviced. The more time that is spent with the bike, understanding how it works, the more instinctive and intuitive its rider will become to real and potential problems. Essentially, routine maintenance is a preventative measure: you will get better at avoiding problems by examining the bike closely and knowing its exact mechanical condition. The equation is quite simple: the more familiar you are with your bike, the better it will feel and perform.

HOME BIKE MECHANIC
Becoming an able bike mechanic is very satisfying, but it may take a little time. Don't be over-ambitious, and don't be afraid to visit your local bike shop if you need advice or professional assistance.

CLEANING

For cleaning your bike, use a selection of long-handled brushes. Toothbrushes are especially good for reaching awkward intricate parts. Use cloths to wipe away grease and for drying the bike. Thorough cleaning is vital – accumulated dirt is abrasive, and increases wear on parts. So a clean bike makes good economical sense, too.

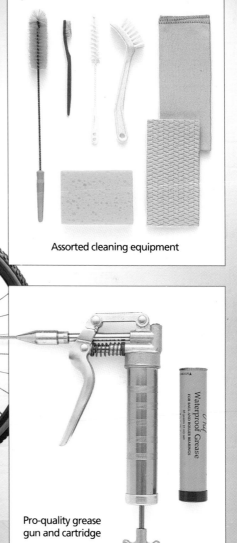

Assorted cleaning equipment

Pro-quality grease gun and cartridge

LUBRICATION

Keep your bike regularly lubricated for good performance and durability. Lubrication reduces friction, prevents parts from grinding or fusing together, and protects against rust. Also, lubricate your bike whenever you clean it.

Cleaning

SERVICING A BIKE can be a much more satisfactory and pleasant task once the bike has been cleaned thoroughly. Cleaning makes bike parts easier to get at and handle, and you will be able to identify mechanical problems more readily. Grime, especially mud and dust, contains tiny particles that are highly abrasive, so regular cleaning following a ride will also help maintain your bike parts in good condition and make them last longer. It is best to develop a methodical approach to a full-scale wash, keeping your hands as clean as possible at every stage; otherwise you will simply transfer grime from one bit of the bike to another. If your bike does not need a full-scale wash, wipe it down with a damp cloth. Always dry and lubricate your bike after washing to avoid rust.

JET-SPRAY WASH

If your bike is very heavily mud-encrusted, which is only likely to be the case if it is a mountain bike, wash it thoroughly with a high-pressure jet-spray hose. Jet-spray hoses are powerful enough to take off transfers, and even paint in some cases, so take care not to stand too close to the bike. Avoid spraying water directly at the bearings, which are sensitive.

Long-handled kitchen brush

SOAPY WASH

For a soapy wash to remove all greasy grime, use a bucket of suds, an assortment of long-handled brushes, and sponges. Help preserve the environment and the bike's wax finish by using a low-alkaline soap or dish liquid, or a biodegradable cleaner such as Bike Elixir Wash & Wax. Start by washing the frame, then move on to more intricate parts of the bike.

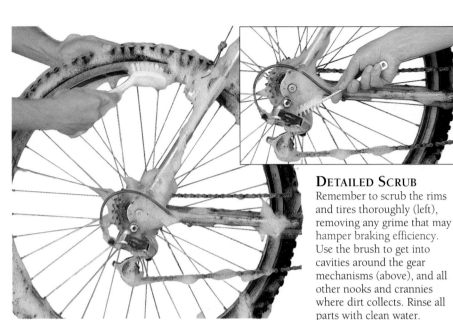

DETAILED SCRUB

Remember to scrub the rims and tires thoroughly (left), removing any grime that may hamper braking efficiency. Use the brush to get into cavities around the gear mechanisms (above), and all other nooks and crannies where dirt collects. Rinse all parts with clean water.

BIKE-SPECIFIC EQUIPMENT

To clean intricate parts of the bike, such as the chain, special cleaning equipment is available from bike shops. However, you can still clean a dirty chain by breaking it and soaking it in a solvent to remove excess grease before washing it with a regular brush. After washing, use a wire brush to remove any stubborn grease. Dry the chain in an oven before relubricating.

FREEWHEEL BRUSH

Freewheels are notoriously difficult to clean, so use a stiff plastic freewheel brush (above) to reach accumulated grease, mud, and grass between the sprockets.

CHAIN BRUSH-BATH

An effective way to clean the chain is to use a brush-bath, such as the Park Chain Bath (left). After attaching the bath to the chain, hold it while you turn the cranks. Brush-baths work best if the solvent and the chain lubricant are from the same manufacturer.

Lubrication

THE TRADITIONAL LUBRICANT, petroleum oil, works well when first applied, but it soon attracts abrasive dirt and has poor resistance to washing away by water. Bikes lubricated with oil need frequent cleaning and relubricating. A far better choice are bike-specific modern lubricants with synthetic ingredients that greatly increase durability and water-resistance (such as Finish Line, Superspray, and Pedros Synlube). Always use a lubricant sparingly and with precision; too much lubricant or grease will attract dirt and increase wear on the parts. Always wipe away any excess and dry the bike thoroughly when you finish. Greases can be either petroleum-based, or synthetic lubricants mixed with a thickener and other performance-enhancing additives. Whatever lubricants you use, never mix them, because incompatible additives can render them useless.

MEDIUM-WEIGHT LUBRICANT
Use a medium-weight lubricant for bushings, which are usually made of brass and include the pivot point pins in the front derailleur and rear derailleur (left), jockey wheels, and any springs holding components in tension. It is important to keep dirt from penetrating bushings, because it will cause corrosion and reduce efficiency. Use the container nozzle to trickle the lubricant directly into the part, and wipe away any excess.

LIGHT-WEIGHT LUBRICANT
Use a light- or medium-weight lubricant for the chain and freewheel sprockets, and to lubricate threads when reassembling components. The quickest and most convenient way to apply a light lubricant is in aerosol spray form. To lubricate the chain (right), simply spin the cranks backward and direct the spray at the moving chain. Wipe off any excess from the outside link plates until they are almost dry to the touch. Also direct the spray at the freewheel sprockets while the chain is moving.

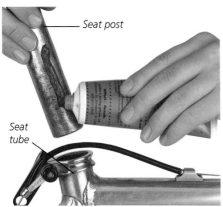

Seat post

Seat tube

SEAT POST LUBRICATION

Remove the seat post (left), then apply grease liberally to the outside of the post before replacing it inside the seat tube. This is extremely important, as the grease prevents the seat post, which is made of aluminum, from fusing with the seat tube, which is in most cases steel. If the components do become fused, it is virtually impossible to separate them. This procedure should be carried out annually. Do the same to the handlebar stem before replacing it in the steerer tube.

BEARINGS

Use grease to relubricate the bearings (the headset, the bottom bracket, and the hubs) after you have dismantled them, cleaned all parts in a solvent, and removed all traces of old grease. A pro-qualtiy grease gun (right) is excellent for the job. Press the ball bearings right into the grease.

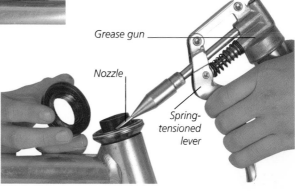

Grease gun

Nozzle

Spring-tensioned lever

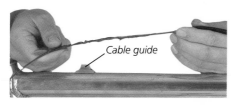

Cable guide

CABLE LUBRICATION

Use grease to lubricate cables (but not Teflon-lined cables) inside cable housing. If your bike does not have slotted cable guides (left), which allow sections of cable housing to slide along the wire, unthread the wire and cable housing completely, then grease and rethread them.

DIY GREASE GUN

A cheap and equally effective alternative to using a pro-quality grease gun is to improvise and make your own. Buy a plastic wide-bore hypodermic syringe (available at most drugstores), remove the needle if there is one, then fill the syringe with grease. Control the flow of grease using the plunger.

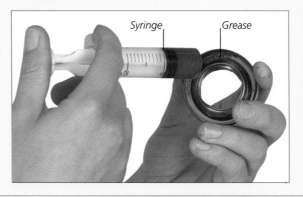

Syringe

Grease

Preparing for a Ride

EVEN IF YOU ARE RELATIVELY FIT and your bike is in top-notch condition, problems can still arise. You should be prepared for all eventualities by carrying a contingency tool kit, a basic first-aid kit, and if you are touring long-distance, various specialist items as well. In addition, make sure you take the right clothes; wear layers that you can remove or put on as the weather changes. A helmet is also highly recommended.

Bandage

Zinc oxide plaster

Adhesive bandages

Safety pins

Frame pump

Multitool

Lint

Scissors

Four-inch adjustable wrench

Tire lever

Puncture repair kit

Roll of electrical tape

Assorted nuts and bolts

Antiseptic cream

BASIC FIRST-AID KIT

Carry a basic first-aid kit even if you are not venturing far from civilization. Injuries should always be treated immediately, and medical help sought as quickly as possible, if needed.

CONTINGENCY TOOL KIT

Always carry a contingency tool kit for roadside repairs, as well as a pump. The kit should be small and light, so it can easily fit into a pocket or saddle pouch.

CO$_2$ CANISTERS

For those keen on "superlite" cycling, CO$_2$ canisters can be used instead of a pump. Canisters act fast (two seconds), making them great for racing and in bad weather. They are not suited to long-distance touring, due to the finite number that can be carried.

Canister and connector nozzle

TOURING

Specialist touring bikes are available, but most bikes, except some road-racing machines, can be adapted to touring use. However, in terms of sheer versatility, mountain bikes are hard to beat for touring, on- and off-road. The F.W. Evans heavy-duty tourer pictured here is a modern mountain bike designed for comfort, stability, and load-carrying. The bike's frame geometry is carefully calculated to minimize the effect of carrying heavy front and rear panniers over long distances.

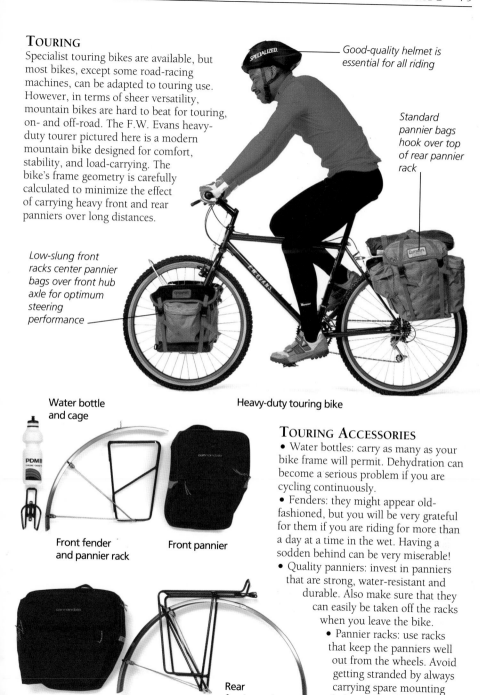

Good-quality helmet is essential for all riding

Standard pannier bags hook over top of rear pannier rack

Low-slung front racks center pannier bags over front hub axle for optimum steering performance

Water bottle and cage

Heavy-duty touring bike

Front fender and pannier rack

Front pannier

Rear pannier

Rear fender and pannier rack

TOURING ACCESSORIES

• Water bottles: carry as many as your bike frame will permit. Dehydration can become a serious problem if you are cycling continuously.

• Fenders: they might appear old-fashioned, but you will be very grateful for them if you are riding for more than a day at a time in the wet. Having a sodden behind can be very miserable!

• Quality panniers: invest in panniers that are strong, water-resistant and durable. Also make sure that they can easily be taken off the racks when you leave the bike.

• Pannier racks: use racks that keep the panniers well out from the wheels. Avoid getting stranded by always carrying spare mounting bolts or clips; heavy loads can sheer them.

Pre-ride Check Drill

BEFORE ANY LONG-DISTANCE ride, a good, systematic check of your entire bike is essential. If the bike is sound, this can be done very quickly. Naturally it will take longer if you discover a problem – and it is best to sort it out now, otherwise you could end up in a real mess later. With practice, you will instinctively know where to start looking for the cause of the problem if something looks, sounds, or feels odd as you are checking.

• **FRAME AND FORKS**
Check frame alignment, and all the tubes for dents and scratches. Examine the forks, checking the underside of the down tube where it meets the head tube. Fractured paint on a steel frame may be a sign of structural failure. A discolored ring on bonded aluminum or composite frames could be caused by glue failure.

• **CABLES**
Check that all cable housing is sound, the cables are not kinked or frayed, and that they move easily and do not slip. Tighten the cable anchor bolts just enough to start denting the wire.

• **RIMS**
Check for trueness: hold a tool near the rim and spin the wheel. More than ⅛ in (3 mm) lateral or vertical movement calls for truing. Ensure the rims are clean and not dented.

• **TIRES**
Check the tire pressure, the tread for wear, and the tire walls for cuts, embedded gravel, or glass.

• **SPOKES**
Test for bends or breaks, and ensure the spokes are evenly tight. On the rear wheel, the spokes near the freewheel should be less tight than those on the opposite side.

• BEARINGS

Check bottom bracket bearings for excess play or binding, and adjust if necessary. Check wheel hub bearings, and tighten axle nuts or quick-release levers. Check headset bearings, and tighten if needed. Check pedal bearings.

• SEAT POST AND SADDLE

Tighten seat post bolt firmly. Tighten saddle clamp securely. This bolt sometimes feels tight when in fact it is still loose; check by trying to move the saddle.

• STEM BOLT

Tighten firmly. The bolt should be tight enough to stay in place when riding, but move if the bike takes a fall. To test, hold the front wheel with your knees and twist the handlebars. Also tighten handlebar binder bolt firmly.

TIRE PRESSURES

Inflate tires to the correct pressure. Under-inflated tires increase rolling resistance and puncture risk. The pressure listed on the tire wall is only a reference point calculated by inflating the tire to twice that pressure without blowing it off the rim. Optimum tire pressure varies according to weight and conditions; experiment, as 5–10 lbf/in^2 (34.5–69 kPa) can affect performance.

• BRAKE LEVERS AND MOUNTS

Tighten mounting bolts firmly. Levers should be tight enough to stay in place when riding, but move in a crash. If a lever feels loose/too tight, adjust the lever pivot bolt.

• BRAKE BLOCK BOLTS

Tighten the mounting bolts firmly. Check the brake blocks accurately meet the rims, with the correct amount of toe-in.

• FREEWHEEL

You should hear a healthy, even, and rapid clicking sound from the freewheel when coasting. Sprocket teeth must not be chipped or bent. Test for damaged teeth by turning the cranks hard in each gear.

• REAR DERAILLEUR

Tighten mounting bolt firmly. Check rear derailleur cable and operate gears to check shifting accuracy and, if included, the indexing adjustment. Adjust if necessary. Tighten pulley bolts firmly.

• CHAIN AND CHAINRINGS

Pedal backward, watching the derailleur rollers for any frozen links. Lubricate if necessary. Check for wear. Check chainrings are true and teeth are not chipped or bent. Tighten chainring mounting bolts firmly.

• FRONT DERAILLEUR

Operate gears to check high/low (side-to-side) travel. Tighten the derailleur mounting bolt and the cable anchor bolt firmly.

• CRANK BOLTS

Test for tightness. Tighten steel bolts firmly. For alloy bolts, first use a steel bolt and tighten firmly, then replace the alloy bolt snugly.

Monthly Service Chart

FOR A WELL-TUNED BIKE, monthly servicing is highly recommended. This consists largely of simple checks for wear, and light lubrication and adjustment. Have all your cleaning equipment, lubricants, and tools on hand, so that if you do discover a problem, it can be dealt with immediately and efficiently. Be methodical and thorough in your approach, and service the bike's components in logical groups. Start by giving the bike a general cleaning, which will make it less messy and much more pleasant to work on.

BRAKES
- Check brake blocks for wear. Remove any embedded grit.
- Check that blocks meet the rims accurately and that toe-in is correct.
- Check brake block mounting bolts.
- Check brake lever mounting bolts.
- Lubricate brake pivot bolts, and tighten as necessary.

CABLES
- Inspect all cable housing for damage. Replace if necessary.
- Clean and examine all cable wires for kinks and frays. Replace if necessary.
- Check for cable stretch or slipping by operating parts concerned (brakes and gears). Compensate for stretching by adjusting barrel adjusters and/or cable anchor bolts.

WHEELS
- Check rims for trueness and even spoke tension. More than ⅛ in (3 mm) lateral or vertical movement requires truing.
- Clean rims and check that they are not dented or dimpled.
- Check each spoke for bends or breaks. Replace if necessary.

TIRES AND TUBES
- Check tire pressure.
- Clean the tires and inspect tire treads for wear.
- Remove any embedded gravel or glass from tread or tire walls.
- Replace overrepaired inner tubes or any with slow punctures.

CHAIN
- Check that chain is not excessively worn or stretched.
- Check chain for frozen links.
- Lubricate with chain lubricant.

CHAINSET

- Clean chainrings and check that they are true.
- Clean chainrings and check for worn or broken teeth.
- Check that crank arms are tight on bottom bracket axle.
- Clean and lubricate freewheel, and check for wear.
- Check freewheel sprockets for worn or broken teeth.

DERAILLEURS

- Check the side-to-side travel of rear and front derailleurs, and adjust travel-adjustment screws if necessary.
- Clean derailleur cages, and lubricate all pivot points and bushings.
- Check indexing accuracy and adjust cable tension at barrel adjusters and/or cable anchor bolts as required.

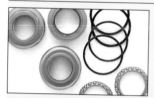

HEADSET

- Check headset bearings for excess play or binding. Make any necessary tightening or loosening adjustments.
- Lubricate headset if grease is broken down or contaminated with dirt.

BOTTOM BRACKET

- Test bottom bracket bearings for excess play or binding. If you have adjustable cup-and-cone bearing assemblies, tighten or loosen if necessary.

HUBS

- Check front and rear hub bearings for excess play or binding. If you have adjustable cup-and-cone bearings, tighten or loosen if necessary.
- Tighten hub axle nuts and quick-release levers.

PEDALS

- Check that pedal bodies are not cracked.
- If pedals are loose, tighten the mounting bolts firmly.
- Inspect toe clips for damage, and toe straps for fraying. Make sure the buckle cannot slip.
- Check pedal bearings and adjust if necessary.

GENERAL

- Apply wax or polish if necessary.
- Check frame alignment and all the tubes for dents or damage.
- Check that every bolt and nut is secure, even if you have used thread adhesive. Tighten bolts with the right tools, and with caution; alloy bike parts can be damaged by overtightening.

Annual Service Chart

ONCE A YEAR, YOUR BIKE should be completely overhauled. This involves stripping down all the components, cleaning, replacing parts when necessary, relubricating, and reassembly. Some components, such as bottom brackets and hub bearings, may require specialized tools available only at a bike shop, but the majority of these tasks can be accomplished using simple tools. One good trick is to break down complete overhauls and integrate them into your monthly service: pedals one month, brakes the next, then derailleurs, and so on.

BRAKES
- Lubricate brake pivot bolts and bushings.
- Strip down and clean front and rear brakes, and brake levers.
- Replace brake blocks if necessary.
- Reassemble brakes, checking that blocks meet the rims accurately and toe-in is correct.

CABLES
- Dismantle all cables. Replace damaged cable housing or frayed or kinked cable wires.
- Grease cables inside cable housing and reassemble, but do not grease Teflon-lined cables. Tighten cable anchor bolts just enough to dent the wire, and fine-tune using barrel adjusters. Test cable tension by operating parts.

WHEELS
- Check rims for trueness and even spoke tension. More than ⅛ in (3 mm) lateral or vertical movement requires truing.
- Clean rims. Replace any that are dented or beyond repair.
- Check each spoke for bends or breaks. Replace if necessary.
- Take wheels to a bike shop to be trued if necessary.

TIRES AND TUBES
- Remove any embedded gravel or glass from tread or tire walls.
- Replace tires with excessively worn treads or tire walls.
- Replace overrepaired inner tubes or any with slow punctures.
- Check tire pressure.

CHAIN
- Replace chain if it is excessively worn.
- Check chain for frozen links.
- Break and remove chain, and soak it in solvent to clean. Alternatively, use a chain brush-bath. Replace chain and lubricate with chain lubricant.

CHAINSET

- Check chainrings and freewheel sprockets for wear. If replacement is required, replace all chainrings, freewheel sprockets, and the chain together.
- Check that crank arms are tight on bottom bracket axle.
- Check that freewheel operates smoothly. If it sticks or sounds rough, replace it. Lubricate.

DERAILLEURS

- Disassemble front and rear derailleur bodies and cages, clean all parts and relubricate. Replace worn jockey wheels.
- Reassemble, adjusting side-to-side travel and position of derailleurs in each gear position correctly.

HEADSET

- Disassemble upper and lower parts of the headset and clean all parts. Replace and grease ball bearings.
- Reassemble and check adjustment.

BOTTOM BRACKET

- Disassemble bottom bracket, clean all parts, replace and grease ball bearings. Replace worn-out cassette bearings.

HUBS

- Strip down front and rear hub bearings, clean all parts, replace and grease ball bearings. Replace worn-out cassette bearings.
- Tighten hub axle nuts and quick-release levers.

PEDALS

- Replace cracked pedal bodies.
- Disassemble pedal bearings, clean all parts, replace and grease ball bearings.
- Replace damaged toe clips or frayed straps.
- For step-in pedals, clean and relubricate step-in mechanism, and check tension setting.

GENERAL

- Check frame alignment and all the tubes for dents and damage.
- Remove and regrease seat post and handlebar stem to avoid parts fusing.
- Wax frame and components (but not wheel rims).

Emergency Repairs

IT'S THE MOMENT ANY cyclist dreads: you are out on a ride and one vital piece of equipment breaks without warning. If you are out in the wild on a mountain bike, you could be in a real mess. Try a little ingenuity – the solution may be closer than you realize. In fact, the list of quick fixes for bike emergencies is endless. All they require is a little imagination: most things can be fixed by improvising with found objects.

• **BANDAGED SADDLE**
If the saddle padding is shot, wrap a shirt or sweater around the seat and secure it with a piece of string.

• **LOST GEAR**
For a broken derailleur, leave the chain on a middle cog and strap the derailleur with a cord to keep the jockey arm extended and the chain taut.

• **TIRES**
If your progress is being hampered by a slow puncture, remove the inner tube carefully from the tire, then wrap some electrical tape around the leaky spot.

• **BROKEN CHAIN**
If a link pin disappears, insert a twig or wire through the link holes, and bind it with tape or cloth. Expect to rebind it every half-hour or so, but it will keep you going.

• **PATCHED PEDAL**
If a pedal body shatters but the axle survives, rebuild it with wire, or make a substitute pedal out of wood. If the axle breaks, lash a piece of wood to the side of the crank.

• Split Saddle

When a saddle splits down to its frame, the choice is between riding standing up or fixing it. If there is any padding left, bandage the saddle with cloth and tie it.

• Brake Lever

If one of your brake levers snaps, force a short, hollow piece of plastic tube over the remaining lever stump, and secure it with some tape.

• Headset Bearings

If conditions are muddy or you ride through a stream, protect the bearings by sliding a section of split tube around the base of the head tube.

• Snapped Straddle Wire

The straddle wire and any sections of brake cable wire that are not threaded through cable housing can be replaced with taut lengths of string if they get frayed or break.

• Front Derailleur

If it breaks, remove the cable and the mechanism, and move the chain to the middle chainwheel.

• Stuff It

Every cyclist should carry a pump, but the odds are that you will be without one when you need it most. Artificially reinflate the tire by filling it with grass or leaves, thin flexible branches, or even old newspapers.

• Temporary Patches

Modern skinwall tires are thin, and if the casing gets badly gashed, it can leave a hole big enough to let an inflated tube bulge through. The trick is to line the hole with some thin material: bits of cardboard, old inner tube, tree bark, even gum wrappers. Then reinsert and inflate the tube.

• Cables

If you damage the cable housing channel on a gear lever and the cable flops out when you use it, wrap a plastic tie around the housing to keep it in the channel. Plastic ties can also be used to hold components in position.

HOMEMADE TOOL

To improvise a wrench, tie a length of string (or wire) to a flat-sided stick. Wrap the string around the nut or part you want to move; wind the string clockwise to tighten, counterclockwise to release. Brace the end of the stick against the nut, and use the long end as a wrench handle.

Flat-sided stick

String

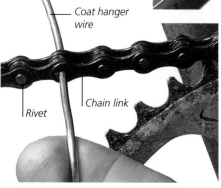

Gear shifter

Zip tie

PLASTIC ZIP TIES

Always keep a supply of plastic ties; they are strong and very useful, especially for attaching parts to the bike frame where mounting bolts have snapped or been lost. Plastic ties can be stored in numerous places on a bike: taped to the saddle rails or to a pannier strut, or concealed inside the seat post.

CABLE MENDS

Broken cables can be rejoined by tying each end to another object, such as a stick, an old tin can, or a length of rag or shoelace. If you cannot rejoin the cable because it has snapped close to the control lever, improvise another means of operating the part by hooking and pulling it over a water bottle bolt on the frame, or some other handy item.

Broken cable

Hole for attaching cable

Coat hanger wire

Rivet

Chain link

WIRE CHAIN RIVET

If you snap a chain and lose the rivet, a piece of wire can hold the links in place. The kind of wire used to make coat hangers is ideal. Run the chain on a rear cog large enough to keep the chain clear of the other cogs, or else the wire may get caught in the space between the cogs. Insert the wire into the empty rivet hole, then cut the wire, leaving 1 in (2.5 cm) or so sticking out each side. Bend the ends backward along the chain, and bind them into place with tape.

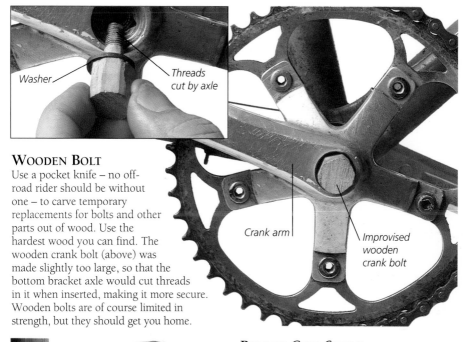

Washer

Threads cut by axle

Crank arm

Improvised wooden crank bolt

WOODEN BOLT

Use a pocket knife – no off-road rider should be without one – to carve temporary replacements for bolts and other parts out of wood. Use the hardest wood you can find. The wooden crank bolt (above) was made slightly too large, so that the bottom bracket axle would cut threads in it when inserted, making it more secure. Wooden bolts are of course limited in strength, but they should get you home.

Solid post

Buckled rim

POTATO CHIP STOMP

After a collision or "wipe-out," any rider can end up with a badly buckled wheel, usually in the shape of a potato chip. Remedy the problem by removing the wheel and holding it with the sections curving away from you at the top and bottom. Place the wheel at an angle against a tree, post, or any solid object. Brace the bottom of the wheel with your foot, grasp the sides curving toward you at three and nine o'clock, and push against them firmly until the rim is straight enough to fit the wheel back on the bike. Use a spoke key to tighten the spokes and true the wheel as best you can. If you do not have a spoke key or adjustable spanner, remove the tire and adjust the spoke nipples with a screwdriver. Ride home very slowly.

Frame Damage

DAMAGE TO A BICYCLE FRAME can be the result of either shock impacts or simply old age and metal fatigue, or a combination of both. Much frame damage is the result of cumulative stresses, so it is important to check for damage as part of your regular servicing, as well as after any serious accidents. Some apparently minor "injuries" can induce much more serious failure later, so pay attention to all frame damage, at least until you have had the bike checked by a qualified frame-builder. You will not necessarily see any cracked paint or crumpled tubes when a frame is damaged, but inaccurate steering is a sure sign. Steel-frames are the simplest to repair, as tubes can be removed and replaced relatively easily and without significant structural consequences. Glued aluminum frames are also easy to repair, in contrast to those that are welded, since reheating the previously heat-treated structure is likely to upset the metal's composition.

Rear dropouts

Head tube

String

Seat tube

Taut string

CHECK ALIGNMENT
Peculiar steering is often a result of a bent frame throwing the wheels out of track. To check tracking, attach a length of string to a rear dropout, wrap it once around the head tube about halfway up, then tie it to the other rear dropout. Make sure the string is taut. Measure the distance from the seat tube to the string on each side with a ruler. Ideally the distances should be identical, but most production bikes are generally off-track by up to ⅛ in (3 mm). Over ⅛ in (3 mm) difference between the two sides indicates a bent frame. Take the bike to a bike shop for professional realignment.

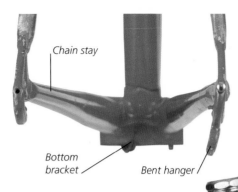

Chain stay

Bottom bracket

Bent hanger

BENT REAR DERAILLEUR HANGER

This can be caused by the rear derailleur hitting the ground or snagging the wheel (due to poor side-to-side travel adjustment: see p.46). This can seriously impede gearing performance, particularly on indexed gearing systems. Steel frames can usually be bent back into shape by a professional; aluminum tends to snap if this is attempted, requiring a welding job. Some aluminum frames have replaceable hangers.

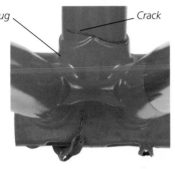

Lug

Crack

Damage to top tube

FRONTAL IMPACT

A serious front-on crash may not bend the front forks at all. On the frame shown here, the forks, which are relatively strong, have survived, but the shock of the impact has been transmitted to the now-crumpled top and down tubes. This kind of damage is not irreparable, but worth the expense of repair only if the frame is fairly valuable.

Damage to down tube

FRAME CRACKS

These generally tend to appear around frame joints, and are a consequence of extreme old age or uneven heating during construction. Steel tubes can be replaced individually if the frame has lugs. A minor crack can be brazed-over to stop it spreading.

OTHER DAMAGE

The only damage likely to cause serious injury is total tube separation – thankfully very rare. Watch for bent forks and cracked seat lugs or joints, which can be dangerous and should be repaired at a bike shop. Stripped bottom bracket threads can be recut at a bike shop too.

STUNT RIDING

Mountain bikes encourage "bunny-hopping" jumps and other stunts that are potentially frame-damaging. Skilled riders absorb impact with their arms and legs, leaving the bike intact. However, without these skills, repeated abuse of this kind will eventually take its toll on the bike frame, and most manufacturers' warranties will not cover it.

Troubleshooting Chart

A BICYCLE IS A DYNAMIC extension of your body. Learn to tune into your bike, so that you automatically listen to it and watch it as you cycle along. The better you ride, the more aware you will become of the bike's mechanical condition. All bikes produce a constant melody of whirs, clicks, and soft hisses that form a rhythymic pattern when all is working well. Listen, look, and feel for unusual noises and riding sensations, and try to track down the source immediately. Use this chart as a rough guide to getting to the root of a problem.

SYMPTOM	LIKELY CAUSE	SOLUTION	PAGE
Knocking or jittering when brakes applied	• Brakes out of adjustment • Forks loose in head tube • Bulge in rim or rim out of true • Brake mounting bolts loose	• Center brakes and/or adjust brake block toe-in • Tighten headset • True wheel or take rim to a bike shop for repair • Tighten bolts	• 24–25 • 60–61 • 32–33 • 25
Brakes do not work effectively	• Brake cables are sticking/ stretched/damaged • Brake blocks worn down • Brake blocks/rim greasy, wet, or dirty • Brakes out of adjustment • Brake levers are binding	• Clean/adjust/regrease/ replace cables • Replace blocks • Clean blocks and rim • Center brakes • Adjust brake levers	• 22–23 • 24 • 25 • 23, 26
Brakes squeak or squeal when applied	• Brake blocks/rim dirty or wet • Brake blocks worn down • Brake block toe-in incorrect • Brake arms loose	• Clean blocks and rim • Replace blocks • Correct block toe-in • Tighten mounting bolts	 • 25 • 24 • 25
Frequent punctures	• Tire pressure too low • Spoke protruding into rim • Tire not checked after previous puncture • Tire tread/casing worn • Inner tube old or faulty • Tire unsuited to rim	• Correct tire pressure • File down spoke • Remove sharp object embedded in tire • Replace tire • Replace inner tube • Replace with correct tire	 • 31 • 34–35 • 34–35 • 34–35
Inaccurate steering	• Headset loose or binding • Front forks bent • Wheels not aligned	• Adjust/tighten headset • Take bike to a bike shop for frame realignment • Check tracking and align wheels	• 60–61 • 32

Symptom	Likely Cause	Solution	Page
Wheel wobbles	• Hub cones loose • Wheel out of true • Headset binding	• Adjust hub bearings • True wheel • Adjust headset	• 64–65 • 32–33 • 60–61
Clicking noises when pedaling	• Loose bottom bracket spindle/bearings • Loose pedal axle/bearings • Stiff chain link • Loose crankset • Bent bottom bracket/pedal axle	• Adjust bottom bracket • Adjust bearings/axle nut • Lubricate chain • Tighten crank bolts • Replace axle	• 62–63 • 66–67 • 40–43 • 52 • 62–63/66–67
Grinding noises when pedaling	• Bottom bracket bearings too tight • Pedal bearings too tight • Chain hitting derailleurs • Derailleur pulleys dirty/binding	• Adjust bearings • Adjust bearings • Adjust chain line • Clean and lubricate pulleys	• 62–63 • 66–67 • 40–43 • 47
Chain jumps off freewheel sprocket or chainring	• Chainring loose • Chainring out of true • Rear or front derailleur side-to-side travel out of adjustment • Chainring teeth bent or broken	• Tighten mounting bolts • True if possible or replace • Adjust derailleur travel • Repair or replace chainring/set	• 53 • 52 • 46, 51 • 52–53
Chain slips	• Chain worn/stretched • Stiff link in chain • Chainring or freewheel sprocket teeth excessively worn/chipped • Chain/chainring/freewheel not compatible	• Replace chain • Lubricate or replace link • Replace chainring and sprockets and chain • Seek advice at a bike shop	• 40–43 • 40–43 • 53, 55, 41–43
Gear shifts faulty	• Front or rear derailleur not adjusted properly • Derailleur cables sticking/stretched/damaged • Indexed shifting not adjusted properly	• Adjust derailleurs • Lubricate/tighten/replace cables • Adjust indexing	• 50–51/46–49 • 44–45 • 48–49
Freewheel does not freewheel	• Pawls are jammed	• Lubricate. If problem persists, replace freewheel	• 55

Glossary

A

Aerodynamic drag The resistance of air to the movement of an object; the combination of a) pressure drag – the resistance from low pressure zones behind a shape, and b) friction drag – when the layer of air next to the surface of a vehicle separates from it.

Airfoil (aerofoil) A structure that has a streamlined profile to reduce drag.

B

Barrel adjuster Barrel-shaped knobs through which cables pass – used to fine-tune the adjustment of cables to take up or give slack; can be turned clockwise or counterclockwise. Barrel adjusters are located on the brake levers, gear shifters, and front and rear derailleurs.

Bearing cartridge/cassette Sealed unit containing lubricated ball or roller bearings. Disposable and virtually maintenance-free, cassettes can be fitted to the bottom bracket, hubs, and pedals.

Belt drive Friction-grip belt, sometimes with notches for added grip. Clean, but inefficient and expensive.

Bosses Brazed-on mounting points on a bike frame for bolting on items such as cantilever brakes, down-tube gear levers, and pannier racks.

Bottom bracket shell The part of a bicycle frame that accommodates the bottom bracket bearings (adjustable components or a sealed unit) and axle, onto which the cranks are threaded. The shell is threaded on the inside.

Brake block Rubber or synthetic shoe that engages with the braking surface of the wheel rim to stop the bicycle.

Brazing Process of joining two pieces of steel tubing together using a non-ferrous alloy such as brass, which has a lower melting point than the metals being joined.

Bushing A sleeve or tube on which a part, or parts, rotate.

C

Cable guide Brazed-on or riveted to the bike frame, cable guides keep cables in position as they pass along the tubes and keep them from hitting the rider's body or any other parts of the bike.

Cadence Pedaling rate, measured as the number of crank rotations per minute. Tourers and commuters pedal at 55–85 rpm, racers from 95–130 rpm, depending on conditions.

Caliper brake Two hinged arms. Pulling the brake cable activates a pincerlike movement, forcing the brake blocks to engage the wheel rim.

Cantilever brake Two separate brake arms that pivot on bosses brazed onto the frame. A straddle wire connects both arms, and cable tension is centered at the straddle yoke, so both arms are activated simultaneously.

Chainset Collective term for the cranks and the chainrings.

Cleat A device for locking a shoe and pedal together. A cleat is a small plastic or metal plate that is permanently attached to the sole of a shoe. The cleat is designed to engage positively with the pedal.

Crank Lever arm joining the pedal to the chainwheel and bottom bracket.

D

Down tube The tube that connects the head tube to the bottom bracket.

Drag See *Aerodynamic drag.*

Dropouts Slots at the front and rear of the bike for holding the wheel axles.

Drum brake See *Hub brake.*

F

Ferrule Alloy component that fits onto the end of a section of cable housing to prevent the housing from becoming frayed when secured in a cable stop brazed onto the frame.

Flange Circular collar projecting from each side of a wheel hub, with eyelets into which the spoke ends are secured.

Frame set All the tubes that make up the frame of a bicycle.

Front derailleur Front transmission mechanism (generally cable-activated) that guides the chain up or down between the inner and outer chainrings.

G

Gauge Thickness or diameter.

Gear ratio On a bike, the gear ratio measures the number of sprocket rotations per one chainring rotation. One rotation of a chainring with 48 teeth will cause a wheel with a sprocket of 12 teeth to rotate 4 times: a gear ratio of 4:1.

Groupset A typical groupset includes the following components: chainset, freewheel, hubs, gear shifters and derailleurs, brake levers and brake mechanisms, and bottom bracket axle.

H

Headset Divided into two parts at the top and bottom of the head tube, the headset contains the bearings on which the steering tube rotates.

Head tube Tube in which the steering tube rotates by means of the headset bearings. The head tube angle can have an affect on steering performance.

HPV Human-Powered Vehicle. Technically, a bicycle is an HPV. In practice, the term is used for any human-powered vehicle that is not a bicycle.

Hub brake A drum and shoe device, which brakes the wheel at the hub as opposed to the rim.

Hybrid Term given to a street bike design that fuses together key features of a mountain bike and a touring bike: straight handlebars, bar-mounted brake and gear levers, cantilever brakes, and wheels with narrow-section multipurpose tires.

I

Indexed shifting Cable-activated gear changing system in which gears correspond with given points marked on the lever mechanism. The system requires accurate adjustment of the front and rear derailleurs to work effectively.

L

Lugs Sleeves that correctly position two tubes together for the purpose of joining by soldering or gluing. Frequently decorative, lugs add strength by providing more surface area for the glue or solder to grip, and for distributing the stress on the frame.

P

Pawl Pin that engages a notch or notches in a ring.

Play (or excess play) Term used to describe looseness in a bearing assembly, characterized by clicking sounds.

Q

Quick-release clamp Used in place of a nut or bolt so that parts of the bike (wheels and saddle) can be easily removed.

R

Rear derailleur Rear transmission mechanism (generally cable-activated) that guides the chain up or down between the freewheel sprockets, or cogs.

S

Stem Attaches the handlebars to the frame via the steering tube. The size of the stem determines the fore-and-aft position of the handlebars.

Spoke nipple Component onto which the end of a spoke threads, and which tensions the spoke against the wheel rim when tightened using a spoke key.

Straddle wire Short length of cable anchored to both brake arms of a center-

pull, or cantilever, brake. The cable passes through a straddle yoke to which the brake cable is attached. When the brake cable is pulled, force is distributed equally to each brake arm via the straddle wire.

T

TIG-welding A type of welding process in which metal tubes are heated until they melt and fuse together. The harmful effects of oxidization are prevented by tungsten inert gas being constantly directed at the join that is being welded.

Top tube The tube connecting the head tube to the seat tube. Usually horizontal on racing bikes, the top tube is often angled downward on mountain bikes to give the rider more clearance.

Torque Any twisting force or power that causes rotation.

Tracking The alignment of front and rear bicycle wheels relative to each other.

Transmission A system that transmits power from the operator (human or mechanical) of a vehicle to the wheels to produce forward movement or drive.

Travel Term describing the extent of movement in a particular direction. The lateral (side-to-side) travel of the front

and rear derailleurs is limited by travel-adjustment screws.

Treadle drive A system designed to drive a machine by means of a lever operated by foot. The foot movement is linear, rather than circular like pedaling.

W

Wheelbase Distance between the wheel axles on a bike, or where the tires touch the ground. On conventional bicycles, wheelbase ranges from 38–44 in (96.5–111.7 cm). Also associated with wheelbase are trail (the distance a wheel axle follows behind the steering pivot point; the pivot point is where a line down the head tube intersects the ground) and rake (the offset of the axle or fork end from the steering pivot line). Increasing rake decreases trail. Less trail gives more sensitive handling. More trail gives less responsive steering, but greater stability.

> ## MEASUREMENTS
> Cycling convention dictates that mountain bikes are measured imperially, road and touring bikes metrically. Exceptions to this rule include the cranks, which are always measured in millimeters, even on normally imperial mountain bikes.

Index

Index continued

ACKNOWLEDGMENTS

Dorling Kindersley would like to thank: James Walters at Covent Garden Cycles; F. W. Evans at The Cut, Waterloo; Richard Bucknall and Victoria Gibbs (Jane Stockman's photographic assistants); Simone Dearing for design assistance; Mike Grimmer for transporting props; Lol Henderson for hand modelling; and Peter Moloney for the index.

Picture Credits: (Key: *l* – left, *r* – right, *t* – top, *b* – bottom, *c* – center)
All commissioned photography by Philip Gatward except for the following by Jane Stockman: p.20 *r* (all), p.21 *tl*, *bl*, p.22 Anatomy (all), p.23 (all except *tr*), pp.24–25 (all except *cb*, *br*), p.27 *cb* , p.28 *cr*, p.29 *tl*, pp.30–31 (all except *br*), p.33 *tr*, p.38 *cr*, p.39 *tr*, *tl*, p.41 *tl*, p.43 *tr*, *tl*, pp.44 *tr*, p.45 *br* (both images), pp.46–47 (all except *br*), pp.48–49 (all), pp.50–51 (all except *br*), p.52 *tr*, *c*, p.53 *bl*, p.54 *tr*, *bl*, p.55 *tr*, p.57 *t*, p.58 *r*, *l*, p.59 *r*, *l*, p.62 Anatomy (all), p.63 *cb*, *br*, p.64 Anatomy (all), p.65 (all except *tl*), p.67 *cb*, p.69 *tr*, *br*, p.70 *br*, p.71 *tr*, *tl*, pp.72–73 (all), p.74 *br*, pp.78–79 (all except p.78 *b* and p.79 *b*), pp.80–81 (all except p.80 *b* and p.81 *b*), pp. 86–87 (all except *cb*), pp.90–96 (all).
Illustrations on p.24 *br*, *bl* by Janos Marfy.